The Soul and Its Instrument

Additional courses in this series include:

The Nature of The Soul

Corrective Thinking

The Path of Initiation, Vol. I

The Path of Initiation, Vol. II

Leadership Training

Esoteric Heart Center Instruction

Printed editions of some of the above works are available through Wisdom Impressions.

II

The Soul and Its Instrument

Volume III

The Path of Initiation

By Lucille Cedercrans

Wisdom Impressions
Whittier, CA

The Soul and Its Instrument
by Lucille Cedercrans

Second textbook edition (1st soft cover), October 1995

Wisdom Impressions is a group of students and practitioners of The Wisdom. Our mission is to help create the appearance of The Wisdom as a recognized field and Teaching the Wisdom as a recognized profession.

Wisdom Impressions
P.O. Box 6457
Whittier, CA 90609-6457

ISBN 1-883493-21-8 $18.50

IV

The publishers gratefully acknowledge the contributions, over many years, of the groups and individuals whose efforts made this edition possible.

The Great Invocation

From the point of Light within the Mind of God
Let light stream forth into the minds of men.
Let Light descend on Earth.

From the point of Love within the Heart of God
Let love stream forth into the hearts of men.
May Christ return to Earth.

From the center where the Will of God is known
Let purpose guide the little wills of men —
The purpose which the Masters know and serve.

From the center which we call the race of men
Let the Plan of Love and Light work out
And may it seal the door where evil dwells.

Let Light and Love and Power restore the Plan on Earth.

"The above Invocation or Prayer does not belong to any person or group but to all Humanity. The beauty and the strength of this Invocation lies in its simplicity, and in its expression of certain central truths which all men, innately and normally accept — the truth of the existence of a basic Intelligence to Whom we vaguely give the name of God; the truth that behind all outer seeming, the motivating power of the universe is Love; the truth that a great Individuality came to earth, called by Christians, the Christ, and embodied that love so that we could understand; the truth that both love and intelligence are effects of what is called the Will of God; and finally the self-evident truth that only through *humanity* itself can the Divine Plan work out."

Alice A. Bailey

VI

Editors' Foreword

The Soul and Its Instrument is part of a series of courses on self-initiated spiritual growth and development. These courses are designed to facilitate step-by-step unfoldment from individuality to group awareness and conscious service to the One Life. This conscious service is called the path of discipleship, and those who walk this path are called Disciples.

The courses prepare the student for the inner work of the Disciple. This inner work is accomplished through meditation which is the creative activity of the Soul or consciousness. Thus, each of the texts in this series is a course in the art and science of meditation.

The first incarnation of *The Soul and Its Instrument* was in 1953, as 18 loose-leaf lessons. These lessons formed the third volume of *The Path of Initiation Series* of courses. This series (with related works, such as *The Nature of The Soul* and *Corrective Thinking*), was designed to be taught to small classes and (eventually) at or through a school of The Wisdom.

The loose-leaf version of the course was taught to classes in Washington State during the early and mid-1950's, and in California in the late 1950's and early 1960's. The first bound editions were published in 1995.

The Soul and Its Instrument is a course of instruction in The Wisdom, an independent field of study, experience, and practice.

The text occasionally mentions *Corrective Thinking* and *The Nature of The Soul*. At the time this text was written, volumes one and two of *The Path of Initiation Series* (of which this text is volume three) were called *Corrective Thinking* and *The Nature of The Soul*. Both of those courses were rewritten in the late 1950's, producing much larger and very different works with the same titles. Thus, the text refers to the shorter, early versions that are also part of *The Path of Initiation Series*.

The editors have (wherever possible) replaced gender-specific pronouns with gender neutral or gender inclusive pronouns. These adjustments place the text in closer alignment with the overshadowing intent.

The editors also corrected a number of minor punctuation, grammar and spelling errors, and have used the British style of punctuating quotation marks.

Table of Contents

Directory of Techniques

The inner disciplines listed below are an essential part of *The Soul and Its Instrument*. Like all such disciplines, they are designed to produce specific effects in the consciousness, bodies, and environment of the student. When these disciplines are practiced in the proper order and manner, they facilitate unfoldment from individuality to group awareness.

Combining these disciplines with drugs, or other techniques, or using them for selfish purposes, is dangerous. We strongly recommend that you eliminate all substance abuse from your lifestyle and approach this course (and the techniques) with the intent to make your persona a better instrument of service.

LESSON 1

Introduction To Group Work

Group Responsibility to
the World Group and Humanity,
Individual Responsibility to the Group,
Assessment of Motivations for the Work,
Identity: Personality, Soul and Creativity,
Habits and the Recognized Need
for Discipline and Application

LESSON 1

Most of the individuals who receive this second series of instructions are those who have become integrated into a group of "minds" who are dedicated to the work of the Soul. They have in the first series become acquainted with the immediate goal insofar as their own development is concerned and are earnestly working toward that goal.

For the sake of those who may still be on the borderline between searching and realization, I shall here define the immediate goal of such groups in a two-fold manner as follows:

1. Group Responsibility to the World Group and Humanity:

The group as a whole realizes its purpose as service. For this purpose it has been conceived and born; for this purpose it continues to grow.

The group realizes that it is not alone in this endeavor, but that it is really a portion of a larger group whose experience and consciousness is such that it is actively engaged in service to the race.

It recognizes that at the head of this World Group stands the Christ and His senior disciples, those who constitute the teachers and guides of the race.

The small group, actually in the state of infancy, then recognizes its responsibility first to the larger group of which it is a part, and then to humanity. It endeavors to align itself with the world group and its teachers, conforms to the higher ideals as represented by the Christ, and slowly expands the periphery of its consciousness to include the World Group. It then becomes a channel for the energies pouring down from the Soul to a needy humanity.

During this same period of expansion the group as a group is confronted with several different kinds of choices: its type and method of service activity, its membership size, its methods of procedure, etc. It must learn to differentiate between that which is important and that which is not, as well as how it is best adapted to serve.

Thus the group passes Initiation and becomes an integral part of the World Group of Servers.

2. Individual Responsibility to the Group:

This is the stage in which I now find most of you. You are just beginning to recognize your responsibility to your group, which is the development of the instrument to its highest point of efficiency, and integration with the other members of the group.

Remember again, the purpose of the group is not your attainment. It was not created to serve you as an individual. Its service is to humanity as a whole and your growth is your own responsibility to the group. Think on this. It is important.

Most of you are now ready to receive technical in-structions that will enable you as a group to enter into more definite service activities. You are aspirants and probationers on the Path of Discipleship leading to Initiation.

Others of you may not as yet have entered into outer group activity. In that case you are studying and working alone insofar as physical plane awareness is concerned, and in some ways yours is a more difficult task than the others.

Lesson 1

If this be the case, take time now to realize that you are a member of the World Group of Disciples (if only as a probationer). Consider the connotations of this fact and proceed as though you were a member of a group meeting regularly on the physical plane. Consider your responsibility to such a group and rest assured that as soon as you are ready you will find your co-workers.

I should here like to insert a bit of advice to all of you. Consider your motives. If there are any of you who are members of the group for any reason other than those described in the preceding paragraphs, drop out until such time as you can and do accept the teaching as Truth and until such time as you definitely feel a desire to serve. Those who do not meet with these two requirements will find the second series very difficult, if not impossible, unless the study proceeds as a scientific investigation with the investigator remaining completely detached and impersonal. My brother, your time will come, and with it the joy of recognition. Until such time, go your way in peace and take with you the love and understanding of your brothers.

To the rest of you, I, on behalf of my brother disciples, welcome you into the White Lodge. Together we stand as one, dedicated to the Christ and the work of the Father. In the name of the Christ may you receive the blessings of the Father and in receiving, share those blessings with all mankind. Peace be with you.

As you have no doubt observed, the second series is subtitled "The Soul and Its Instrument". I wish to speak of this before continuing with the technical instructions covered in this series.

At the end of the first series students are inevitably confused if asked to explain their identity. "Who and what are you" serves to bring the student into a state of bewilderment. This is good in that it forces an issue at the

The Soul and Its Instrument

proper time and students must sooner or later consider their true identity.

They have by this time become aware, at least in part, of their essential duality. They have for a long time been aware of themselves as personalities, identified with form. In studying the first series of instructions, "The Nature of the Soul"[1], they have become aware of that which underlies form, the Soul or consciousness aspect, and are attempting to identify themselves with that. At the end of this second series[2] they will have shifted their polarization and realized that they are the Soul, independent of the form though utilizing it as an instrument of contact with this, the physical plane.

Then let us presume, for the purpose of this series, that we are Souls, my brothers. We are not personalities aspiring to the Soul, but rather we are Souls aspiring to the Christ and attempting to control the personality.

In order to better do this, let us clarify what is meant by the term "personality". The personality is a reflection of all past experience into which the Soul has entered while incarnate in form. In other words, the aggregate of individual experience is reflected into a more or less integrated form, that form constituting the personality. It is a conditional state of existence into which the Soul projects a part of its consciousness for the purpose of further experience. It is not a state of consciousness as is supposed. Therefore, the term "personality consciousness" is, in a sense, a misnomer. What is actually meant is that the projected consciousness has identified itself with the personality rather than the Soul and has then recognized and accepted the limitations of the personality as its own.

---

[1]The Path of Initiation, Vol. II. An earlier, short version of The Nature of The Soul.
[2]The Path of Initiation, Vol. III. The Soul and Its Instrument.

6

Lesson 1

The projected consciousness is the creative aspect of the Soul. Its many successive lives in form finally bring it to an understanding of the Law of Cause and Effect. Once it is no longer identified with the personality, its incarnations become acts of service to the race. By this time it has developed its own nature, its inherent characteristics and its own quality.

I stated previously that this series of instructions is designed to shift the polarization of the student out of the instrument into the Soul. This is done through a process of identification and the exertion of a positive control over the form nature. This, of course, necessitates discipline.

At the same time the student is engaged in the evocation of creative activity. The basic need of all individuals, after they have reached a certain stage of development, is the need to create. The inability to satisfy that need is the cause of many of our psychological problems today. The individuals for whom these instructions are written fall into this category.

If you have properly analyzed yourselves you have become aware of a great lack within your experience. That lack, when seen from the right perspective, lies within yourselves. You may be able to pin it down to a lack within some part of your equipment; the physical, emotional or mental. This is because there has been no true alignment of these three, and no one-pointedness of purpose. The desire nature has often been at war with the physical or mental aspects or both, and in most cases this battle is focused primarily between the desire nature and the mental aspect, with the physical body taking the place of the battleground. It shows the effects of this battle in many ways and is often badly scarred as a result. The desire nature must be dominated and controlled by the consciousness focused in the mental aspect. It must be made to aid the consciousness in its creative activity and this is only possible through self-

The Soul and Its Instrument

imposed discipline.

What are your habits and in what aspect are they rooted? Any habit is now undesirable because it holds the consciousness a slave to the form nature. Almost any habit is rooted in the desire nature. Many so-called physical habits are rooted here. The desire nature is compensating for some unfulfilled wish. Just so long as this condition remains, full Soul consciousness is not possible.

Knowledge of this poses a test for students, does it not, a test of their sincerity, a test of their strength and a test of their motives?

I do not order you to discipline yourselves. I merely offer suggestions that point out the way. I do advise you to begin now with a process of identification. The "I" consciousness is an aspect of the Soul. It is not, then, its physical body, its desire nature or even its mental aspect. These are temporary and are discarded often for newer and better equipment. It is not necessary, however, to discarnate in order to build better equipment. It can be done while incarnate and at some time it must be done during this cycle. That is part of the evolutionary process. The aspirant masters the form nature while inhabiting it and this usually takes many lives.

In the light of this, my brothers, I suggest that you contemplate identification, discipline and application.

Before proceeding with this series, I shall ask you to quickly review the first series. As an assignment, determine for yourselves the discipline indicated by the instructions received and the response both your consciousness and your form nature have made to them. Give this in written form to your teacher before you proceed with further lessons, and keep a copy for yourselves.

PEACE BE WITH YOU

Lesson 1

Notes

The Soul and Its Instrument

Notes

_____

_____

_____

_____

_____

_____

_____

_____

_____

_____

_____

_____

_____

_____

_____

_____

_____

Lesson 1

Notes

LESSON 2

The Constitution Of The Human Entity

The Monad,
The Soul or Consciousness Aspect,
The Personality,
The Threefold Movement
of Manifestation,
Further Clarification of
the Monad, Soul and Personality

LESSON 2

In this lesson we shall begin our study of the constitution of that entity called humanity. This will provide the basis from which to proceed to eventual understanding of the threefold human entity and its utilization in the working out of the Divine Plan.

We shall break down the human atom, as it is called, into its three major aspects. Since you have at present no method of proving or disproving that which I shall communicate, I ask you to proceed with an open mind accepting for the present the following information as a hypothesis with which to experiment. As your experiments develop you will be able to prove the truth in experience. Remember that reality only becomes factual as it is worked out on the physical plane in concrete form.

As regards your experimentation, proceed with extreme care, experimenting only along those lines indicated in these lessons, and only after you have sufficient information to warrant experimentation. Remember that knowledge without understanding can be dangerous. I rely upon your good judgment, ability to follow instructions and your right motive.

The three major aspects of the human atom are:

1. The Monad.

This is the positive central life that is characterized by the Will to Be. Its motion is forward progression, its force is propulsion and its quality is defined as being electrical.

You may or may not have heard of Monadic consciousness. We shall attempt to clarify the term, but any attempt to bring understanding of this state to your present state of consciousness is almost futile. It is the

The Soul and Its Instrument

consciousness of the One rather than the many, having nothing whatsoever to do with form as you know form. Monadic communication as such does not exist. That which is termed "Monadic communication" is the interpretation the Soul gives to Monadic impulse; and even that word "impulse" carries different connotations than does the term as used by present day science.

The plane that is known as Divine Mind is the home of the Monad, and this plane, too, is most difficult of definition. It lies above the Divine Plan and yet it is the perfect plan. It lies above thought and yet it is the perfect thought. It lies above form and yet it is the perfect form. From this formless One proceed the many. From this unconscious state proceeds the states of consciousness.

I realize that this does not mean much to most of you and yet seeds must be planted and will in time germinate.

2. The Soul or consciousness aspect.

This has been defined so many times and in so many ways and yet still I find little understanding among you. The Soul is the conscious thinking entity indwelling the human form. It is the neutron, that which experiences, that which absorbs and that which radiates. Its motion is spirallic, its force is radiation and its quality is love or pure reason.

The Soul is consciousness and we find it in many different stages. Everything that is — is animated by life; the nature of that life being some degree of consciousness and resultant activity. I am not here speaking of self awareness for that is only one state of consciousness. The rock, the vegetable, the animal, the human are all conscious. The human has awareness of self. Concentrated into the human atom are all the stages of awareness — some developed, some latent; thus humanity is created in the image and likeness of God Himself.

16

Lesson 2

3. The personality.

We spoke of this in the first lesson of the series as being a conditional state of existence into which the Soul focuses itself.

It is related to the negative electron that is characterized by activity. Its motion is rotary, its force is repulsion and its quality is relativity.

In considering these three major aspects I shall give you three words upon which to meditate for further clarification:

1. Monad   —   Synthesis
2. Soul   —   Magnetic attraction
3. Personality —   Relationship

Each of these three aspects is also a triplicity and for purpose of study should be broken down into their three component parts. This I shall do for you. However, I do not expect you to understand or even grasp the significance of that which is imparted at this time. Simply file it away for future reference.

1. Monad
   a. Will or motivating impulse
   b. Love or synthesis
   c. Intelligence or activity

2. Soul
   a. Spiritual or super human, referred to as the Christ consciousness
   b. Human
   c. Animal or subhuman

3. Personality
   a. Mental
   b. Astral or emotional
   c. Physical or etheric

The Soul and Its Instrument

Let us now consider these three major aspects from a little different angle, that of energy and motion. We have three distinct types of energy moving in three major patterns in three frequency ranges. It is the pattern of movement, and, of course, the frequency that determines the form any body of energy will take.

Monadic energies move in a straight line forward, thus we have evolution.

Solar energy moves in a spirallic pattern, thus we have the development of consciousness.

Personality energy moves in a rotary pattern, thus we have experience.

Time and space as we know them are phenomena of personality energy.

Affinity or attraction is a phenomenon of Solar energy.

Progress is a phenomenon of Monadic energy.

For contemplation I shall list certain further manifestations of the three types of energy as they are stepped down and work out on the three planes of human endeavor:

Monadic	Soular	Personality
Synthesis	Magnetic Attraction	Repulsion
Progress	Awareness	Change
Inspiration	Intuition	Instinct
Eternity	Creation	Time and space
Will	Love	Activity
Power	Wisdom	Knowledge
Cosmic awareness	Universal awareness	Self awareness
Continuity	Life	Death

18

Lesson 2

Though all of this may not seem clear to you now, once again I ask you to file it away for future reference. Disciples must learn to think in terms of energy before they are initiate. Later you will relate this information to other information and understand much that is now only vague and difficult. In the meantime, try to realize that you are an aggregate of many energies manifesting in a world of energies and reacting to the impact of many energies upon your own energy body. It is your direction and control of your quota of energy that determines your evolution of consciousness and its consequent experiences.

Today we find the human entity entering into that stage of development wherein some of the Laws of the Soul begin to govern experience. This is because of certain Soul energies that are pouring down into race mind consciousness and stimulating spiritual awareness.

That these energies are misinterpreted and wrongly directed is true, but this is ever true as new energies make their presence felt. A transition period always manifests and precipitates a series of crises in which the entities concerned must make a choice and so determine the path they will take.

Now, as never before in the history of the race, the opportunities for group service to a needy world are great. Groups united in purpose can lift humanity out of the darkness into the light if they so choose. Whatever path humanity takes will have been the result of group decision. Think on this.

How is that decision made? You may well ask this question, for it is not made suddenly and in the twinkling of an eye. It is made daily as disciples put into activity those energies that are theirs to direct. Those energies we shall consider as three-fold for the moment — mental energy, emotional energy and physical energy. As disciples accept, embody and radiate Truth consciously, and with the goal in mind, their decision is made and the forces of light are strengthened. Every word which is impulsed by Divine Love, and formed with a clear mind, brings the Christ consciousness that much closer. Every act of selfless service swings humanity onto the path.

Lesson 2

Notes

The Soul and Its Instrument

Notes

_____

_____

_____

_____

_____

_____

_____

_____

_____

_____

_____

_____

_____

_____

_____

_____

_____

_____

_____

Lesson 2

Notes

LESSON 3

The Threefold Instrument Of Contact
And The Etheric Network

The Four Major Energies
of the Etheric Body,
The Seven Centers or Chakras
of the Etheric Body,
Meditation on the Etheric Body

LESSON 3

In this lesson we shall study the instrument of contact through which the Soul must work while incarnate. I shall have to speak generally and in broad outlines in order to cover this very large subject in a few short lessons. Much, then, will not be given and will have to be filled in later through study and meditation, as well as experience.

I would suggest that you learn to enter that meditative state known as contemplation in order to arrive at an understanding of these lessons. Most of the material given can be defined as seed material. It is up to the student, and time, to nourish the seed to growth. This must always be the pattern by which spiritual truths are given to insure the protection of those who are not ready for revelations. Though the time is now when much can be revealed which has heretofore been hidden, it must necessarily follow the tried and true methods of projection. In this way the safety of the many is assured.

The instrument of the Soul is three-fold in nature, being composed of three energy bodies co-existent in time and space. These energy bodies are:

1. The Mental
2. The Astral
3. The Etheric

I have not listed the dense physical body because it is not a principle. It is a temporary effect of very short duration when observed from the perspective that sees the evolutionary scheme as a whole. It is an appearance or effect of the etheric, which we shall consider now in more detail. The etheric network is the vital energy body that feeds and makes possible the life of the dense body. It interpenetrates all substance, relates it and holds it in form. It is electrical in nature, being composed of many tiny lines of force, which form channels for the flow of energies throughout its entire system. In the human form these lines of force underlie and are peculiarly related to the physical body and nervous system. From here the etheric body interpenetrates every atom of the physical body and extends out some inches from it, varying in distance according to the evolution of the consciousness concerned.

It is composed of many classifications of energies, four of which we shall consider here:

1. The sum total of energies that govern individual form. It is the type of etheric energy that makes a person an individual. It relates the particles of substance to one another and the central life, causing the emergence of an integrated whole — possible of intercommunication, conscious direction and coordinated activity. Without this underlying network the human form would fall apart. In cases of poor integration or gaps between the etheric and the physical — we see the feeble minded, imbecilic, etc. The indwelling entity has no adequate contact with and, therefore, no control of its dense body.

2. The sum total of energies underlying and governing the environment of which the individual is a part. This energy relates people to their families, associates, their locale, and makes possible most of their daily activities. This energy is not confined to individuals in the same manner as are the former energies but interpenetrates the environment in which they live, move and have their being.

3. The sum total of energies that interpenetrate and influence the nation or peculiar race. The resulting relationships are obvious.

Lesson 3

4. The sum total of energies which interpenetrate and govern the planet itself and relate humanity to everything therein.

A study of the above energies will bring a picture of at-one-ment underlying the appearance of separation. This picture is very important to the student. Therefore, I would advise you to dwell upon it deeply and often.

The physical body depends entirely upon the etheric for its appearance of action. It is the etheric network underlying the brain and nervous system that carries the subtle stimuli so necessary to human activity but rarely considered by the average psychologist. It is the carrier for the mental energy, astral energy and physical force. Through the medium of the etheric network the mind impresses the brain. Through this same medium the astral body (desire nature) impresses the brain and nervous system. Through this same medium the force necessary to action is fed into the physical body via the nervous system and the endocrine glands. When the etheric body is sufficiently developed the Soul utilizes it to dominate and control the mental nature, the astral consciousness and the physical body.

The etheric body contains within it certain force centers that can be defined as centers of transmission for incoming and outgoing energies. Of the many centers in the etheric network, we shall consider here the seven major centers and their functions. These are located in the etheric network that extends outside the physical and from there interpenetrate the physical counterpart.

I shall very quickly list these seven major centers and their obvious function in order that you may arrive at a picture of the etheric body itself. This information is given for consideration but not for experimentation as yet. Please keep this in mind.

The Soul and Its Instrument

1. The head center is located from three to six inches above the top of the head, extending down into the head itself. It is the center that puts the lower consciousness in touch with the spiritual Soul and in most cases is relatively quiescent.

2. The ajna center is located between the eyes from three to six inches outside the forehead and extending into the forehead. This center is relatively quiescent until such time as the three-fold personality becomes more or less integrated and can be consciously focused on the mental plane. At this time the center is activated and plays an important part in the alignment of Soul, mind and brain. It relates the three in awareness and aids in the creation of a magnetic field of mind so important to the growth of a student's understanding. This magnetic field of mind is used by the Soul and the disciple in service to the race.

When the disciple nears the 3rd Initiation, an interplay of energy is set up between the head center and the ajna which compels the entire system to reorientation. This last statement is important to those of you who find yourselves in the process of becoming adjusted to the head polarization.

3. The throat center is located from three to six inches outside the body, about midway in the neck. It is very active within the intellectual — although not conditioned and influenced by the two head centers in most cases. Therefore, all mental types who concern themselves with concrete form with little or no spiritual understanding are influenced by energies reaching them via this center, and in turn exert influence via the same center. Very often such individuals are very narrow minded regarding things that do not

Lesson 3

demand their interest; not having the insight characteristic of the active ajna. They are normally methodical, intolerant and critical. When this center is dominated by the head and coordinated with the ajna center, we see individuals who display a great potential for good, who are dependable and very capable and who are almost always a powerful influence within their particular sphere of influence. They will invariably use words as a medium of influence, but in a manner totally different than is the case with lesser evolved individuals.

4. The heart center is located from three to six inches outside the spine between the shoulder blades and extending into the body. This center is an extremely important one in that it feeds the physical body with vital life energies via the physical heart and the blood stream. It also relates the individual intuitively and as a Soul with the Soul of all others. Energies pouring in via this center impel the individual to seek, to establish relationships, and to aspire.

A very interesting correspondent can be drawn here for those who can intuit. The heart center corresponds to the physical sun, that which provides the conditions conducive to growth. Think on this.

This center, like all others, must be dominated by the head center and coordinated with the ajna to be effective in service. When an alignment between the head, ajna, throat and heart takes place, a human becomes a creator. In the creative artist of today we usually see an alignment of the head, throat and heart. When the ajna center becomes the coordinator, we shall see creative works that will surpass anything known today insofar as influence is concerned.

5. The solar plexus center is located from three to six inches outside the spine just above the waist. This center is active within most of humanity today, particularly all of those who are emotional types. An over-active solar plexus is responsible for all astral phenomena of lower and sometimes higher nature. It has eventually to be dominated and finally superseded by the heart center.

6. The sacral center is located from three to six inches outside the spine, about three inches below the waist. This center transmits the creative energies to the reproductive organs and has to be dominated and superseded by the throat center.

7. The Kundalini center is located from three to six inches outside the spine, just above the coccyx. This center is the last to be awakened and is lifted to the ajna center at the 3rd Initiation. Very little can be given about it at this time as the consciousness of the race does not warrant the revelation of its mystery. It is analogous to the Virgin Mary and is esoterically called the Latent Fire of Matter.

In order to clarify this instruction I shall list once again the centers with a word symbol of their functions.

1. Head center .... Divine Will

2. Ajna center .... Divine Love-Wisdom

3. Throat center .... Divine Intelligence

4. Heart center .... Life

5. Solar Plexus center .... Form

6. Sacral center .... Propagation

7. Kundalini center .... Appearance

Lesson 3

I shall here give an exercise that will stimulate awareness of the etheric and at the same time better the health of the physical.

1. Focus the consciousness in the ajna center and align with the Soul.

2. Visualize the etheric network underlying the physical body.

3. Then extend the "I" consciousness from the ajna throughout the etheric body that interpenetrates the physical. Do this slowly and carefully.

4. When the "I" consciousness has been fully extended into the etheric, speak the words:

   "My etheric body is revitalized and energized".

5. Withdraw the consciousness back into the ajna and speak the words:

   "My physical body is galvanized into right action."

As an assignment, write a report of the results of this exercise and hand it in to your teacher.

The Soul and Its Instrument

Notes

_____

_____

_____

_____

_____

_____

_____

_____

_____

_____

_____

_____

_____

_____

_____

_____

_____

Lesson 3

Notes

LESSON 4

Three Major Classifications
Of Soul Consciousness

Spiritual Soul, Human Soul
and Animal Soul Defined,
The Dual Nature of the Concrete Mind,
Observing the Mental Process,
The Four Stages of Human
Development Visible Today

Lesson 4

The etheric body is the substantial form of the Soul, acting as a vehicle for the three major classifications of Soul consciousness. They are:

1. The Superhuman or spiritual Soul Consciousness, which is focused into the center of the head, in the region of the pineal gland, via the head center. It is this that relates people to God, making them more than human.

2. The human soul consciousness, focused into the heart center and related centers. It is this that relates people to people and makes them more than animal.

3. The animal soul consciousness, focused in the solar plexus and related centers. This center of consciousness relates humanity to the animal and its past.

As can be easily deduced from the above, these three centers constitute three major centers of contact with consciousness. This contact is registered in each of the three centers and carried to the brain in the manner peculiar to the major classification of consciousness concerned:

1. Spiritual Soul.

Contact with superhuman consciousness in the head center and impressed upon the brain via the etheric network as inspiration.

2. Human Soul.

Contact in the heart center with the group (both the

mental and astral consciousness of the race) and impressed upon the brain via the etheric network as intuition.

3. Animal Soul.

Contact with subhuman consciousness in the solar plexus and impressed upon the brain via the etheric network as instinct.

There is another center of contact that is rapidly developing in the West today, and which is presenting both an opportunity for and an obstacle to, spiritual unfoldment. This center is the throat center which puts humanity in contact with the concrete plane of mind.

While it is not my intention to discuss the mental plane as yet, I shall, however, explain the dual nature of the concrete mind, in order that the student may see the part the throat center is playing in the evolutionary crises today:

1. The concrete plane of mind is that part of race mind that contains all concrete knowledge achieved by the race to date. That so-called knowledge may be correct or incorrect, a truth or a partial truth, or a truth so distorted by its form as to be considered a falsity.

2. The concrete plane of mind is composed of mental matter of sufficient density to clothe an abstraction and so give it concrete form.

The student who has developed this center of contact, and once again there are many in the Western world, has free access to all knowledge that has evolved to the present, as well as an ability to work in mental matter.

This presents a great opportunity for Western students,

in that they can, if spiritually oriented, bring their mystical vision into manifestation on the physical plane. They will not only be dreamers and so-called thinkers, but they will give their dreams form and the race will benefit. The veiling of truth that has been so predominant in the past will give way to a clear enunciation of truth.

The obstacle lies in the fact that where there is a rapid development of this center without spiritual orientation, students become crystallized in their thinking. They contact only concrete knowledge, only that which has been given form by other minds, and in so doing, lose touch with the reality underlying form. This is extremely important and I ask you to give it much thought. The majority who receive these lessons fall into this stage of development and many of them are not as yet sufficiently oriented to contact anything other than concrete form.

Observe your mental processes. Do you think in abstractions or concrete form? Later in this series I shall point the way to freedom from domination on the mental plane by concrete knowledge. In the meantime, prepare yourselves for this step by attaining an open mind. Wherever your thought is set, you are crystallized. Wherever you entertain a set of ideas as being absolute truth, there you are crystallized and incapable of contacting reality; your vision is distorted. Attain an open mind anent all subjects. This is the first step toward the attainment of Wisdom.

We see humanity in many stages of development today, but they can be classified into four major types:

1. The stage in which people move, think and have their being in the animal consciousness of the race. This is rare; however, it can be seen operating in some.

In this stage the solar plexus center, the sacral center

and related centers are highly developed as the main centers of contact. The brain is impressed with impulses coming in through the solar plexus and the sacral. The emotional nature will be of a very low order, meaning there are few real emotions present. The instinct to self-preservation and propagation of the race will be the dominating influence in the life of such a one.

The etheric network with its lower centers, and the dense physical body below the diaphragm will be of a low order, more animal than human, transmitting but dull emotion into the feeling aspect of the person.

During this stage the heart and throat centers will be very slowly activated so that in the latter part of this development the individual will show a tendency to feel emotionally and to respond in a dull sort of way to thought.

2. The stage wherein people move, think and have their being in the strictly human consciousness. This is more preponderant than any other stage at this time; most of humanity having awareness of its emotional relationships both to people and to things.

In this stage we see the solar plexus and sacral development plus an activated heart center, and some activation of the throat. It is here that the emotional nature of humanity makes its rapid development. The astral body achieves great capacity for feeling pleasure and pain, good and bad, etc. Here we find the so called good and bad people of the race — strictly emotional types responding to life according to the impact of their environment upon this emotional response mechanism.

As a result of heart activation, a bridging in the etheric network takes place between the solar plexus with its animal soul and the heart center with its human soul.

Lesson 4

At the end of this stage of development, the animal soul and the human soul will be integrated and functioning as one. The astral body will be highly developed, capable of great emotional depths and highly aware of itself as a center of influence.

3. The stage wherein a person is shifting from the human to the spiritual consciousness. This development is the second largest insofar as membership size is concerned and at this time almost equals the second stage.

Both mental and emotional types are included here, hence much confusion. These people are undergoing an almost constant change of values, are fluctuating in response between the purely form side of their natures and the idealistic. Thus we see the cause of the present world crisis and the constant chaos manifesting.

In this stage the former center of development is seen, plus greater heart activation, throat activation and some ajna activation. The bridging is taking place between the human soul in the heart and the Spiritual Soul in the head, via the mental body. The astral body is undergoing discipline and losing its position as the center of influence to the mental body. The head center is slowly being awakened and transmitting the energies of the Spiritual Soul into the system. The mental body is then the midway point and aspirants take their stand here via the ajna center. Their intuition is functioning, they are becoming attentive to inspiration and are preparing themselves for service.

At the end of this stage the mental body will be integrated with the astral and physical bodies via the etheric network and its system of centers. The bridging will have been done and the two lower states of consciousness will be absorbed into the spiritual Soul.

The Soul and Its Instrument

4. The stage wherein people constantly function in the spiritual consciousness of the Soul. This is rare; however, it is becoming more possible of attainment and can be seen on the verge of emergence in greater and greater numbers.

The seven centers will be fully awake and vibrating in harmony. The polarization will have shifted into the causal body and from here the Soul will utilize the three lower vehicles as instruments of contact within its sphere of service.

Remember that the physical brain is impressed via the etheric network from the center or centers most active. A careful observation of your own response to life will bring you a realization of your center development as well as indicate the necessary steps to be taken toward further development.

As an assignment, please write your understanding of your own center development and the steps you feel you should be taking toward further Soul unfoldment. See how this checks with the disciplinary measures you have ascertained as necessary and hand a copy of the paper in to your teacher.

PEACE BE WITH YOU

Lesson 4

Notes

The Soul and Its Instrument

Notes

Lesson 4

Notes

LESSON 5

The Planetary Etheric Body
As A Vehicle Of Synthesis

States of Awareness,
The Threefold Personality and
the Need for Integration,
The Etheric Body as
the Medium of Communication,
Meditation for Cleansing the Mental Body

LESSON 5

In Lesson 4, I stated that the etheric body acts as a vehicle for the three major classifications of Soul consciousness. Actually it is much more than a vehicle for it coordinates and synthesizes all states of consciousness into one.

A state of consciousness is a state of being aware, resulting from the experience of life in form. A flower is aware of warmth, light and growth; the animal is instinctively aware of things outside itself and the sensations of hunger, fear, etc. Humanity is more or less intelligently aware of itself.

All of these states of awareness, plus many more, we find contained within and functioning through the planetary etheric body. While each one appears as a separate entity, it is in reality but part of the One Life linked to every other part and to the central directing Will of the One Life.

The evolutionary scheme, then, as far as the human mind can grasp, can be seen to be the ultimate synthesis of all states of consciousness within the one body. It has been stated elsewhere as being at-one-ment complete with individuality. In other words, individual awareness of at-one-ment or continuity.

The planetary etheric body is the major instrument of synthesis for this evolutionary activity.

To bring all of this down to individuals and their practical application of Universal Law, we find contained within their etheric network many states of consciousness in the process of integration. I have already listed the three major classifications of Soul consciousness. Now we shall consider the three states of personality consciousness that are the result of the identification of the Soul with form.

The Soul and Its Instrument

1. Mental
2. Astral
3. Physical

It is these three which pose for humanity the greatest problem today. The work of synthesis cannot continue until individuals have integrated their mental, emotional and physical awareness into a working unit. Then their integration with the Divine consciousness, with time, or their past, and with their immediate environment, can proceed as planned.

When aspirants have arrived at the stage of development in which they are aware of their etheric network and are learning to utilize it intelligently, the process of integration goes forward rapidly.

The first step toward this development is, of course, the ability of students to accept and contemplate the fact of the etheric body. They must realize that everything they see, hear, taste, smell and feel are the result of energy being carried by and focused through the etheric network. All energies that they receive come to them via this medium as well as all energies which they project. That which they sense is the effect of this inner activity.

The energies that continually flow through the etheric network originate on the plane of mind and are directed by the entities found inhabiting that world.

The spiritual Soul "in meditation deep" sets into motion the Divine ideas which in their turn are consciously or unconsciously received and incorporated into the mental life of the personality, as the thoughts that direct the flow of energies through the etheric network. The ability of the personality to receive, correctly interpret and apply these Divine ideas will determine the condition of its etheric vehicle. Where the idea is distorted into thoughts containing greed, resentment, fear, etc., a

Lesson 5

clouded, sluggish etheric instrument will result; hence an unhealthy physical body and an unpleasant environmental condition.

When one stops to consider the thought life of the average individual and the race as a whole, it is little wonder that the world is engulfed in pain and suffering today. This will not, cannot change until the thought life of the human family has changed. It is the duty of all aspirants and disciples to cleanse and purify their thoughts as well as bend all of their efforts toward the purification of racial thought. When hate and resentment give way to love and forgiveness, when desire and greed give way to right aspiration and service, then we shall see the era of Christ.

Once again I seek to warn the earnest student. This is not done through criticism. Disciples endeavoring to cleanse the thought life of themselves and their environment do not do so by sticking their noses into another's business. They do so through self discipline, first of all, and through their ability to love their brothers.

My brothers, cease your useless criticisms, your little jealousies and petty gossips. Those who think loving thoughts, who speak kind words and are gentle in behavior are true disciples although they may never have heard of the Path.

I shall now give you an exercise that will aid in the purification of the mental body. I ask that each one of you continue to use this exercise until such time as you, yourselves know it is no longer needed.

Become relaxed and comfortable. Focus the consciousness in the ajna center. From this point of observation let the mind wander for 15 minutes. Do not repress any thought that comes to mind or allow yourself to become alarmed. Simply follow the thought to its logical conclusion.

The Soul and Its Instrument

At the end of the 15 minute period visualize the light of the Soul pouring down into all these thoughts, whether so called good or bad. Hold the mind steady in the light and repeat the words:

"The Light of my Soul cleanses, purifies and reveals. I am that Light."

Lesson 5

Notes

Notes

Lesson 5

Notes

LESSON 6

The Astral Body And
The Emotional Nature, Part 1

Three attitudes which hinder growth;
Fear, attachment to phenomena,
and refusal to recognize the astral plane;
The astral body as the power factor
of manifestation

Lesson 6

We come now to that part of the instrument that has perplexed so many occultists and of which there has been very little teaching projected. I am speaking of the astral body and the emotional nature of humanity. Most of the teaching that has been given anent this aspect of the personality has been either misrepresented, misinterpreted or totally confused.

This has been due to several factors, among them an overall lack of understanding regarding the three-fold personality and the lack of proper terminology with which to define it. The terms "astral body" and "astral plane" have been used to define any subtle body or plane seen or sensed by the sensitives. The astral body has been confused for the mental body, etheric body, the Soul, Angels or Devas, Saints, Masters, etc. Many of those who have partially grasped the Truth have rejected the entire plane as total illusion and blithely gone their way ignoring it.

Today, those of us who teach find an appalling condition present within the consciousness of our students; one that is hindering the desired unfoldment of spiritual powers and knowledge. This condition is characterized by three attitudes that I shall explain as follows:

1. Fear of the astral plane that renders the student incapable of dealing with this part of their nature or environment. This fear — which is the product of incorrect teaching, deliberate falsehoods and centuries of superstition — results in an illusion so great as to blind the student to reality. They can reach no further for Truth because they are barred from it by their own fear.

How can this fear be conquered? By first realizing that you

The Soul and Its Instrument

have nothing to fear except that which lies within your-self. Nothing from without you can harm you. This may sound as if it were a statement in direct contradiction to fact, but if you will think deeply you will grasp the concept. That harm that appears to come from another individual or circumstance finds its point of origin within your own consciousness.

The fears of this kind entertained by most people are stimulated by unhappy experience undergone upon the astral plane. For the sake of clarity, let us look into the nature of such experiences and their natural consequence.

In lesson 8 of the Nature of the Soul[1] series I stated: "The astral plane contains the aggregate of human emotion and has been called the world of illusion, for here in form are all of humanity's thoughts concretized and made manifest. All of these thoughts live and have their separate existence on the astral plane. Little wonder it has been called the plane of illusion. Wise must be the consciousness who enters and works therein."

Consider, then, individuals who for the first time find their awareness focused in this world. They will be aware in that area that contains the forms either created or entertained by themselves and those within their environment. If these individuals entertain fear of any kind, they will meet the object of their fear in form. If they believe in a devil or a hell, they will very likely see a devil complete with horns and a tail and a flaming hell of brimstone and fire. If their thoughts are largely ugly with jealousies, resentments, etc., they will meet them in form; without recognizing them as their own creation. Those within their environment who are closely related to them will also furnish this world with their created forms. The individual will then see and

[1] The Path of Initiation, Vol. II. An earlier, short version of The Nature of The Soul (also by Lucille Cedercrans).

Lesson 6

hear dreadful things that are a threat and a danger to them. They will see them as a reality of the astral plane; never recognizing them as their own created world, subject to their domination. This, then, will constitute their illusion; the fog that veils the light of Truth.

The aspirant must cultivate fearlessness. Aspirants must accept first the fact that they are their only enemy. They no longer look upon others with fear and suspicion. They realize love for all and so establish right relationship. They turn the light of the Soul upon their instrument and the surrounding environment, effecting the purification of the various aspects of their consciousness. Such ones will not be fooled by the forms contacted on the astral plane, but will know and coordinate their activities with the reality underlying it.

2. Attachment to phenomena, which serves to hold the student a prisoner to the world of form. This attachment ensues when the student contacts the astral plane without the adequate understanding to correctly interpret the astral form, and without sufficient knowledge to handle the forces contacted therein. Students think they have reached the goal in the beauty of the form and strive no longer for spiritual perfection, but are led into the by-path of phenomenal experience of unduly long duration.

Such individuals will have behind them many incarnations of devoted and often fanatical aspiration; their consciousness will be focused in the astral nature and their experiences will be largely emotional. Their vision of perfection will naturally constitute a form of great beauty and intricate design. In their meditation they will contact their astral body, which will be highly emotional and of great strength. The sensory centers of their brain will be stimulated in such a way as to register the sight and sound of their inner astral visualizations

The Soul and Its Instrument

(those forms that they have created during centuries of devoted thought). They will not recognize the form as their personality creation, but will accept it as the goal, hence the streets paved with gold, the angels with harps, etc., of many Christian religions. Such ones no longer aspire; they live in a dream world, content with its outer appearance of beauty and are deaf to the call of service and a needy humanity.

Later individuals may develop a certain psychic sensitivity to other forms on the astral plane; but because their attention is caught by the form they will be incapable of correct interpretation. They will be the recipient of astral force without the ability to handle it. They may have visions, hear voices, foretell the future, etc., but there will be little of spiritual significance in what they do. Their inability to handle astral force will gradually lead to a deterioration of the instrument, resulting often in disease, insanity and death.

This attitude constitutes one of the greatest dangers to all aspirants. Therefore, I say to you — do not look for phenomena. Do not concentrate upon the development of psychic sensitivity. Wait until you have acquired an understanding of Truth. As your spiritual perception is developed there will be a parallel development of extra sensory perception that will be utilized with Wisdom. If you do register a vision, hear a voice, etc., attach no importance to it. Look for truth in abstract form. Later you will be able to give it concrete form, without losing touch with reality. Then yours will be a gift of interpretation and service to the race.

3. Refusal to recognize the existence of the astral plane, which causes students to inhibit their own emotional nature, closes the door to extra sensory perception and makes it utterly impossible for them to engage in creative activity.

Lesson 6

The astral body and plane is the power factor in manifestation. Until it is understood, controlled and properly directed, the student cannot engage in creative work. Astral energy gives the mental form the substance that ensures its manifestation in physical form. This is true of any work of art as well as the service rendered to humanity.

The student who refuses to accept the astral plane as anything other than complete illusion, usually does so because they have seen how fear of and attachment to it have blinded others to truth. They are mentally polarized and usually contemptuous of emotionalism. They are determined to avoid the mistake of their brothers and so consider the entire subject of the astral body and the emotional nature as false. They inhibit their own emotions, thereby aiding in the growing though hidden strength of their own created forms and their emotional impact. They seek to work solely upon the mental plane, building form after form that they must meet sooner or later upon the astral plane.

Because of this attitude their thought-forms cannot take material form; therefore, they are frustrated in all of their attempts to manifest Truth in the world in which they live.

All of these attitudes delay the necessary integration of the three-fold instrument and ultimate Soul awareness.

I shall ask each of you to eliminate from your minds all of the preconceived ideas you have accumulated anent the astral plane before continuing with the next lesson.

Dare to throw out all of the so-called "knowledge" you have acquired and begin the study of this subject with a fresh uncluttered mind.

Notes

_____

_____

_____

_____

_____

_____

_____

_____

_____

_____

_____

_____

_____

_____

_____

_____

_____

Lesson 6

Notes

Notes

Lesson 6

Notes

LESSON 7

The Astral Body And
The Emotional Nature, Part 2

The astral plane as a convergence
of many forms, worlds and energies;
The individual astral body
and its contact with the physical body;
Three methods of cleansing the astral body;
Inherent dangers of past systems
and the astral body;
A mantram for truth

Lesson 7

The astral plane is composed of energy that interpenetrates and duplicates physical substance. It lies between the frequency ranges of the mental and physical planes and is held in relation to, and coordinated with, the other planes via the etheric network. Its substance is molded and vitalized by the energy of thought — meaning that not only does every physical form have its duplicate upon the astral plane, but that every mental form also has its duplicate there. It is, then, insofar as outer appearances are concerned, a world in which there are many worlds, a plane of many varied forms.

The disciple who has attained true vision looks beyond the form and sees a plane of converging forces. These disciples see that which is coming from higher levels into incarnation and that which is coming from lower levels out of incarnation, plus the force of human emotion. They see those energies and forces in action that decide human destiny and in so doing, are able to see into the future. This seeing into the future is not as some suppose a viewing of the form, but rather of the conditions that are both in a state of present precipitation and probable future precipitation.

They see the path both in symbolic form and in present conditions. They may visit, as a part of their training, the many illusory worlds existing upon this plane (such as the wish life of an individual, a family, race or nation, the different hereafters created by the various religions, the many so-called occult schools that are attended by those both in and out of incarnation, etc). They are not, however, blinded by the form they see. They are able to look upon it and interpret its meaning; its place in the scheme of things. In doing this they are not attracted by the glamour of the form and are free, then, to observe, learn and move on to the next lesson. They are neither alarmed or elated by what they see and are gradually enabled to control the forces contacted upon this plane for the betterment of humanity.

When disciples have reached this stage of development they are a great power in the world for good; free and uncluttered by the glamour of the astral plane. They can safely lead others in truth, for their light will pierce the fog that would ordinarily blind them.

The individual astral body interpenetrates and duplicates the physical body and environment. It will be colored by the individual thought life and be composed of the grade and quality of energy determined by the evolution of consciousness concerned. The astral or emotional nature, whether of an advanced or lesser evolvement, expresses the quality of the personality consciousness. Individuals are known by their emotions. Whether or not they will be successful in their undertakings is dependent upon the development of their astral nature. To be successful one must be equipped with emotional depth. This does not mean that the individuals are given to emotionalism, but that they have the emotional strength to devote their efforts to any given plan.

The astral body underlies and is peculiarly related to the liquid content of the physical body. It has four main points of contact with the physical body, which are:

1. The Sacral center

2. The Solar Plexus center

3. The Heart center

4. A certain area of the brain

The aspirant very rarely contacts the astral plane via the sacral center. Either the solar plexus door has closed or is in a process of closing. They are usually in contact via the heart center — and so becoming aware of their

Lesson 7

karmic relationships. Their aspiration is activating the centers of contact in the brain and they are being unconsciously prepared for the study of and entrance into the astral plane. When these brain centers have been correctly stimulated and activated; when the students have received an intellectual grasp of this plane, and when they have undergone the purification of their own astral nature, then they will develop extra sensory perception as well as other spiritual powers.

Let no students fool themselves into believing that they are ready for this development, until the former development has been made. For just so long as they are subject to emotionalism, to glamour of any kind, and are interested in phenomena — they are barred from this type of growth. The development of psychic sensitivity and other spiritual powers is extremely dangerous if it is either forced or sought after before the student is ready.

No true teachers ever seek to develop the student along these lines, for they know that as the growth of consciousness progresses in the right direction, so will the abilities of the student. These will be a by-product of the student's understanding.

Students are first taught to cleanse their astral aura through:

1. Character building.

They develop those attributes that they know to be their divine heritage by conforming insofar as is possible to their divine prototype, the Soul. This constitutes for them the "ideal", the vision held before the personality as the goal of development. This is necessarily colored by much glamour in the beginning and is usually motivated by selfish interests. However, as the student nears the state of right aspiration, the vision becomes a thing of beauty and conforms more nearly to reality, until, at

The Soul and Its Instrument

last, the aspirant is expressing one or more of these attributes through right action. Usually such a one is engaged in service through creative art, however, as yet they have no true concept of Soul inspired service. They are nonetheless on the path approaching conscious discipleship and will one day wake up to their inner motive.

2. Meditation.

When aspirants consciously enter the Path they are taught the fundamentals of meditation. They learn that through right thought the astral body can be controlled and utilized as an instrument of service. Taking their stand on the plane of mind, they consciously turn the light of Truth into their astral nature. There they see standing the forms of centuries which they have created through many successive incarnations. They learn the meaning of karma, the hidden motives that have driven them as a personality both to success and failure, and finally the secret of the astral body, which is revealed only during a certain initiation.

They are taught the effect of sound upon this aspect of their instrument and through the right use of sound, and the energy of the mind, they rebuild the astral body. They throw out of it all that substance that is heavy and colored with the gross emotions of lesser evolved humanity, and build into it substance of a finer, clearer nature. The astral body then becomes the desire body of the Soul and is utilized as an instrument of magnetic attraction for all that is needed for service.

3. Service.

This activity is in itself the final act of purification, for only through service is the disciple freed from the glamour of the three worlds. Through what appears as the great sacrifice, the chains of the astral plane drop from the consciousness and are seen as the illusion so often spoken of. The disciple has then attained self-mastery.

Because there is much teaching presented today that actually constitutes a danger to humanity at this time, I shall take this opportunity to point out to students certain practices that must be avoided if they are to avoid unnecessary hardship.

1. Do not center the consciousness in the solar plexus center, either through meditation or so-called mental exercises. This center was used during Atlantean days as the main center of contact, by both sensitives and magical workers. The race was emotionally polarized and the evolutionary plan necessitated the stimulation of the astral consciousness.

Today, remnants of that civilization remain with us, and (due to crystallization or deliberate misrepresentation) certain of their teachers are presenting the old Atlantean methods.

The evolutionary plan today necessitates mental polarization and the development of mind. The astral body must be subdued and controlled by the consciousness focused in the mental aspect. This eliminates, for the present, many of the old phenomenal experiences known to mystics — and constitutes one of the sacrifices the human race must make for the sake of progress. It is difficult to give up anything which one has grown to know and love, but believe me, my brothers, this phenomena that holds so many of you prisoners to the astral plane is not reality. It has been a step in the evolution of consciousness. You will note I stated "has been".

2. Do not use the creative energies to produce magical works via the sex act. That such a practice would be taught in the world today is unthinkable, but we have among us those who are doing

The Soul and Its Instrument

just that. The purpose behind this type of teaching I shall not reveal to you, but I warn you that such practices will lead down a path that is most dangerous and undesirable for humanity.

3. Do not attempt to leave the body through any center but the head center, and then, only under instruction you know to be rightly motivated.

Finally, my brothers, I shall give you a mantram to use before you accept any instruction as to meditation, the act of transition, etc., which will, if used with complete honesty, insure your protection against that which you do not as yet understand and cannot, therefore, control.

Focus the consciousness in the head and repeat slowly and with care,

"I seek only the power of Truth."

Lesson 7

Notes

The Soul and Its Instrument

Notes

Lesson 7

Notes

LESSON 8

The Astral Body And
The Emotional Nature, Part 3

The future and the astral body;
Four ways to recognize astral polarization;
Movement from astral to mental polarization;
Methods of attaining mental polarization;
A meditation for group service

Lesson 8

In our last lesson I spoke in very general terms concerning the purification of the astral-emotional nature. In this lesson I shall be more explicit — giving detailed instruction that can be applied in a practical manner to the daily life of any student.

The astral body contains within it all those forms that are eventually to manifest the experiences of the individual. It reflects or distorts pictures created in some mind, giving substance to each picture, so that a substantial form may emerge; whether that form be a situation, a series of events, a book, etc. It is, then, the womb of creative humanity.

Within the astral body of the average person we find those forms that constitute the wish life of the individual. They may be of a very high nature or a very low nature and are a product of many centuries. They are usually created in race mind (which is largely astral in nature) and given individual coloring by the lower mental body of the person concerned. In this case, the polarization is astral — because the astral body is positive to the mental. Individuals are polarized in the astral-emotional nature when:

1. Their own astral body reflects the form predominant in the astral consciousness of the race.

2. They lend their mental energies to the task of fulfilling desire.

3. Their astral body distorts the higher mental picture, as a result of emotional reaction.

4. They respond emotionally to any proposed plan.

The Soul and Its Instrument

The task of all aspirants is to complete the shift in polarization from astral to mental, and then to integrate the three-fold instrument into a working unit. The shift in polarization is not a sudden happening, as some of you are inclined to suppose, but is a slow process of successive steps, carried out over many lives — until the consciousness lives entirely in the plane of mind, directing all activity from there. The task of shifting the polarization and integrating the instrument is simultaneous, so that there is always a balance in the evolution of the consciousness.

One entire lifetime may be spent in shifting the consciousness from one area in the astral nature into the mental body, and the next life spent in stabilizing that shift of polarity. The next life will see the consciousness being lifted from still another area of the astral nature, etc.

When a certain percentage of consciousness has been shifted into the mental aspect, the entire process is speeded up. Many of the former desires have been transmuted into right aspiration and the student then becomes an aspirant. As such, they cooperate with the evolutionary scheme by consciously taking the steps necessary to complete the shift in polarity. These steps are:

1. They become the observer.

I have given you much anent this subject so shall not repeat the instruction here.

2. Through study and meditation.

They learn the nature of emotion. You will remember in Lesson 8 of the 1st Series[1], page 3, I stated, "Emotion is the effect produced by the impact of astral energy upon

---

[1] The Path of Initiation, Vol. II. An earlier, short version of The Nature of The Soul.

86

Lesson 8

the sensory system of the physical body and its surrounding environment. The vibratory impact of that (astral) form upon the sensory system produces what we call an emotion, according to its strength, type and quality".

I would suggest that you go back to that lesson and study again the instruction devoted to the emotions. There is much there of real value.

   3. They impose certain realized disciplinary training over the astral nature as a result of this knowledge.

They endeavor to keep it free of emotion. This they do, not through inhibition, but through right aspiration and love.

They endeavor to pour through their astral nature — Divine Love for all that breathes. Divine Love is not an emotion. It is the Law of the Universe, the energy of which is cleansing and healing.

Right aspiration they achieve through the re-orientation of their desires. Instead of desiring things of the world, they desire, above all else, to live the life of the Soul. As that desire transcends the lower desires, their astral body slowly becomes aligned with and negative to the mental body.

   4. Through meditation they become receptive to the vision of the Plan.

This is one of the most difficult of all the steps, because the student has so many preconceived ideas as to what the Plan is. The moment the term "vision" is introduced, those preconceived ideas crystallize and it is this crystallization that is seen as the Plan. As a result, aspirants enter another by-path and are again delayed until experience teaches them the fallacy of their belief.

The Soul and Its Instrument

In an effort to avoid this error, I shall attempt to clarify what is meant by becoming receptive.

Aspirants must first realize that they could not have truly envisioned the Plan at this stage of development. Any picture that they may have envisioned must be a distortion at best. It could not be otherwise. If this is difficult for you to accept, my brother, you have already entered the by-path. Dare to discard ALL pictures — ALL visions of a so-called Plan, for it is only by clearing and stilling the astral body that the Plan can be reflected as it is. It is only by alerting the mind to the Soul that the Plan can be known as the Soul knows it. The vessel must be emptied in order to be receptive. When this state of receptivity is attained, then the Plan is reflected via the mind into the astral body (the womb) to be later precipitated into service activity. Then, my brother, will the light of the Soul pour forth to a waiting humanity.

I shall now give you a new group meditation, which I shall ask you to incorporate into your meetings, both as a training and as a service. Furthermore, I shall ask that each one of you eliminate your individual meditations, no matter what they may be or how great the sacrifice, and use this one as your daily morning meditation.

1. ALIGNMENT

    a. Become physically relaxed and comfortable.

    b. Become emotionally calm and serene.

    c. Become mentally poised and alert.

    d. Focus the consciousness in the ajna center and realize at-one-ment with the group.

Do this by:

Lesson 8

1. Seeing the etheric network as a clear and unobstructed channel, linking every member to every other member.

2. See the group astral body as a still pool of clear reflecting water.

3. See the group mental body as alert and standing steady in the light of the group Soul.

2. MEDITATION

   a. Meditate 10 minutes on the following seed thought:

      "I, the Soul, know and serve the Divine Plan."

3. DESCENT

   a. As the group Soul, sound the audible Om, pouring Divine Love-Wisdom through the three-fold group instrument, and seeing it radiate Love and Light to humanity.

   b. Keep a daily written record.

Notes

Lesson 8

Notes

_____

_____

_____

_____

_____

_____

_____

_____

_____

_____

_____

_____

_____

_____

_____

_____

_____

LESSON 9

The Mental Body And
The Plane Of Mind, Part 1

Clarification of terminology:
consciousness, mind and mental body;
The threefold consciousness of the individual;
The "individual" mind and
the creation of thought;
The division of the Universal Mind: Divine Mind,
Abstract Mind and Concrete Mind

Lesson 9

In the next few lessons we are going to study the mental instrument. However, before we get into this aspect of the personality, I shall take this opportunity to clarify some of the terminology that has confused so many anent the subject.

The terms "consciousness", "mind" and "mental body" have not been sufficiently defined to present the student with understanding when they are used. This is due partly to the use that has been given them by the race and the inability of the student to intuit the meaning underlying the words. I would remind you once again to pass from the word to its inner meaning. Remember, a word symbolizes a reality and constitutes a doorway into the world of that reality. The ability to pass through the doorway is determined by the development of the intuition. The intuition can be developed by attempting to feel the meaning underlying the form. Instead of accepting an impression that is vague or possibly misinterpreted, become still and allow the consciousness to move into the true meaning. It is most difficult to describe this technique for it is one so little used. It is not an activity of the concrete mind, but rather one of the consciousness. The consciousness or understanding literally moves into the reality.

Consciousness is a state of being aware and is not confined to mental awareness but includes all areas of manifestation. An emotion is an awareness, and therefore, a part of the consciousness. The registration of heat, cold, odor, etc., is a state of awareness that is translated into meaning by the entity concerned. This meaning, then, is a part of the consciousness.

The consciousness, while it is not the entity itself, is an

integral part of the entity and is composed of the essence of all the entity has experienced. It undergoes many expansions, many changes and transmutations, and it constitutes the understanding of the entity.

The consciousness, then, is not the mind or the mental body, nor is it confined to the mental plane. It inhabits all planes of existence and determines the response the entity makes to life in any of those planes.

Consciousness is the result of the merging of spirit with matter. It is the Soul of both and grows to Wisdom as the two continue to merge.

Let us consider the state of consciousness of any individual. It will be divided into three major classifications that I shall explain as follows:

1. That which has been attained in the past and now lies below the threshold of awareness.

This includes knowledge gained during former incarnations as well as that which has been experienced out of incarnation. The surface of this area of consciousness contains that which has been experienced during the present life and has fallen below the threshold of awareness. It can sometimes be recalled. Under proper guidance, the student who is ready can recall experience gained in former incarnations; but this is not advised for any of you at this time nor in the near future.

When the proper development has been reached, the student will achieve continuity of consciousness as naturally as a baby nurses. Do not, therefore, take this by-path into astral glamour.

2. That which lies within the present awareness and is termed conscious knowledge or understanding.

Lesson 9

The extent of this area will be determined by the evolution of the entity and is surprisingly limited. The average conscious awareness includes very little, being limited by the accepted standards of the environment in which it lives. The concept of time and space holds the average awareness confined to but one happening in one place at a time. The identification of the average consciousness with its physical body, confines the awareness to that body and its environment and its consequent limitations, etc.

3. That which lives above the threshold of awareness and includes the consciousness of the individual spiritual Soul, group Soul, Oversoul, etc.

Remember, I have stated elsewhere that the Spiritual Soul is in meditation throughout incarnation until such time as the projected consciousness reaches a certain state of development, after which the Spiritual Soul begins to take an interest in the affairs of the personality. Throughout all of these incarnations, the essence of all experience in form is absorbed into the Divine consciousness as Wisdom, plus the essence of experience achieved on its own plane. This constitutes an area of consciousness that is far in advance of the other two.

It is interesting to note here how little actually lies in the threshold of awareness at any given time and with what rapidity the content can and usually does change. There are those, of course, whose conscious awareness remains practically the same at all times. They have been spoken of as being "in a rut".

The average conscious awareness is in communication with the subconscious almost constantly, and in cases of aspirants and disciples, is in communication with the superconscious. This accounts for the rapid change of content and the gradually increasing awareness.

The Soul and Its Instrument

Mind has been greatly misinterpreted because it is, to the average consciousness, an intangible. Actually, mind is just as tangible as you or I, though not perceptible to our astral-physical sensory apparatus. Mind is a plane of existence, a world in which there are many countries, many environments, etc. It is not consciousness, nor the mental body, but is rather the world in which consciousness, traveling in a mental vehicle, lives, moves and has its being.

There is no such thing as individual mind — and right here is where so much confusion exists. We say a mind — your mind, my mind, etc. I have even used the term in these lessons when speaking of various things "originating in some mind". This is, however, a misnomer; for there is, in reality, only one mind. When speaking in terms of an individual mind, what is actually being considered is the mental body of an individual consciousness.

The mental body, with its sensory apparatus, is the vehicle of contact with the world of mind. The consciousness, through this instrument, contacts (through conscious or unconscious selectivity), accepts or rejects and interprets thought-forms existing in the Universal Mind.

It is utterly impossible for the consciousness to originate or create thought. An abstraction may be given concrete form, after it has been contacted by the consciousness, and it is this we confuse with creation.

A so-called creative mind is actually a receptive mental body, capable of receiving, interpreting and transposing vibration. The individual mental vehicle is apportioned its quota of mental matter with which to mold the proper clothing for the abstraction. This mental matter is concrete mind substance, and though it does exist outside the mental body and cannot, therefore, be called an individual mind, it is theirs with which to work.

Lesson 9

Just as a farmer's plot of ground lies outside his physical instrument and is not separated, in truth, from the rest of the physical world, it is nonetheless his quota of physical substance to do with as he pleases, according to known physical laws. In this plot of ground he may plant his seeds; leaving the sun, the rain and the natural food of the earth to nourish them to growth.

The Universal Mind can be divided into many classifications. However, for purposes of this lesson, I shall limit those classifications to three. Later we shall consider some of the others.

1. Divine Mind.

This is the highest plane of mind possible for the consciousness of the present day person to contact and then, only in theory. It is the natural habitat of the Monad, and contains only that which is relative to the Cosmic consciousness. Nothing in this plane of mind is ever related to form, be it a thought-form or a vehicle of manifestation. Form, as the comprehension of humanity knows it, does not exist except in the three worlds of the personality; therefore, this plane of mind must be defined as formless. Here we find consciousness in a pure state of being, insofar as our consciousness can comprehend "being".

2. Abstract Mind.

This is the natural habitat of the Soul and the highest aspect of mind in which the personality consciousness can function. It is here that the lower consciousness is merged with that of the Soul; the union often referred to as the "marriage in the Heavens". It is here that the consciousness takes Its stand during Initiation. Here it is that It bridges the way between that which is material and that which is Divine. And it is here that It attains liberation from the three worlds of human endeavor.

The Soul and Its Instrument

Emanating from the plane of Divine Mind are those impulses that become abstractions in the abstract plane of mind. Here form as we know it is conceived. That form is perfect insofar as we are concerned, and has yet to become manifest in perfection. Form in the three worlds of the personality is distorted by the consciousness of the personality and is, therefore, in a state of evolution.

3. Concrete Mind.

This is the habitat of the mentally polarized personality and is the lowest plane that can be contacted by the Spiritual Soul. The lower planes (astral and physical) are contacted by the personality, either working on its own or under the guidance of the Soul. In this plane of mind the abstraction takes concrete form as thought and is worked out by the personality in the astral and physical plane as fluidic and solid form.

As an assignment, I shall ask each of you to trace the development of a specific hypothetical form, from its conception on the abstract plane of mind to its eventual manifestation on the physical plane. Hand the paper in to your teacher before going on to the next lesson.

Lesson 9

Notes

Notes

Lesson 9

Notes

LESSON 10

The Mental Body And
The Plane Of Mind, Part 2

The mental body, its form and substance;
Each vehicle occupies the same time and space;
The layers and density of mental substance;
The center (chakra) system and
the layers of the mind

Lesson 10

The mental body is an energy body that interpenetrates the astral and physical bodies and is held in relation to and coordinated with them via the etheric network. It is threefold in nature, being composed of three distinct vibratory types of mental substance that have been called:

1. Concrete Mind
2. Abstract Mind
3. Divine Mind

Actually, as I stated in the last lesson, there is no such thing as an individual mind. However, there is an individual quota of mental substance available to the incarnating entity at all times. Any thought that is visualized in the mind substance of the entity is instantly available to all other entities operating on that particular frequency.

The mental substance, which in total constitutes the mental body, is held in form by the focused thought of the overshadowing Soul. This thought, which is actually the blueprint or framework of the three vehicles, is constant and does not change until it is destroyed by its creator. It is not the mental body but rather the essential cause of its manifestation.

The mental substance that adheres to the focused thought and constitutes the mental body, is in a constant state of change. The focused thought is held steady and into its magnetic field is attracted the mind substance that gives it a mental form. This mind substance is continually passing into, through and out of the magnetic field, being immediately replaced by other mind substance.

The mental body is conditioned by the Dweller in the body according to Its thought habits. It can easily be seen, then, that the mental body is not the perfected form as is the inner focused thought held by the Soul, until such time as the consciousness of the Dweller is merged with that of the Soul.

I would again remind you that all of these bodies occupy the same time and space, but different frequency ranges of vibratory activity. The student would do well to visualize a sphere with a dot in the center. The dot is the incarnating entity, the sphere its vehicles of manifestation. Encircle the dot with four larger spheres and label thus:

1. Causal Body

2. Mental Body

3. Astral Body

4. Etheric Body

5. Periphery or
   Physical Appearance

It will be necessary for you to realize that the symbol does not convey a true impression because the bodies interpenetrate one another, and that within each body is an extension of the consciousness of the incarnating entity. According to the degree of identification of the extended consciousness with its vehicle will be the limitation of said consciousness and the lack of continuity. When the lowest extension of consciousness bridges its awareness with the next extension, etc., continuity will have been achieved and simultaneous awareness on all planes of existence will be maintained.

The mental body is composed of various grades and types of mental substance, according to the evolution of the indwelling consciousness. To fully understand this, consider the physical body. It is composed of various types and grades of physical substance, the blending of which appears as a substantial coordinated form.

Lesson 10

There are many grades of mental substance, ranging all the way from that which intermingles with astral substance and consequently is of a slow vibratory frequency, to that which is so subtle and of such a high frequency as to lie out of the range of human experience.

The outer covering or sheath of mental substance that adheres to and is a part of the mental body is what we have called the lower mental aspect. It intermingles with astral substance and constitutes what has been called by some students of psychology, "the reactive mind". It is composed of those half mental, half emotional impressions that constitute in their entirety the world inhabited by a large percentage of humanity. People who live and operate from this polarization react to situations according to the emotional impact upon their already formulated thought habits. Their family background, educational background, religious background, recognized authority and various opinions provide an automatic response mechanism that continuously reacts to all incoming stimuli. Such a one cannot accept any idea for which they have no response already built in. The idea will simply pass through, seldom being registered by their consciousness. If the idea is forced upon them, they will immediately reject it as false (becoming very frightened and usually antagonistic). The apparent rationality of their reactions will depend entirely upon their built-in response mechanism.

The next layer of mental substance is very little removed from the lower one, for it, too, consists largely of a built-in response mechanism. It is more nearly mental, however, and the person who is polarized here may give the impression of logical thought. Because this substance is somewhat finer and more free of astral content, it is more easily assembled into thought and does not crystallize so rapidly, as does that of the lower sheath. This person will be able to venture out into newer realms of ideas providing they do not oppose their foundation of thought. This foundation will be extremely orthodox and represent some commonly accepted authority. We find many mathematicians here (the mediocre ones) and many physical scientists, teachers of orthodox subjects, etc. They are very exclusive in their thought processes, being unable to relate the differing and apparently separated fields of thought.

The next layer of mental substance found in the mental body is still of the same nature as the above two, but of a much greater flexibility. It is not so easily dominated or conditioned by childhood impressions, has a wider range of selectivity (meaning that it can both receive and hold both concrete and abstract ideas for contemplation), is capable of much greater assemblance and is capable of imagination. Here we find mathematicians, scientists, teachers and artists of all kinds using old worn out ideas in new ways.

These three layers of mental substance constitute the concrete mind aspect of the mental vehicle. Individuals who are polarized:

1. In the first layer receives their impressions in the brain via the solar plexus, heart center and the etheric network.

2. In the second layer receives their impressions in the brain via the solar plexus, heart and throat centers; that which comes in via the solar plexus being conditioned by the heart.

3. In the third layer receives their impressions in the brain via the heart and throat centers and the etheric network. In this case, either the heart or the throat may be the conditioner. However, it is more likely that the two will operate together. This one will have developed a small degree of intuition.

110

Lesson 10

The main center of contact for the concrete mind is the throat center. As stated in a former lesson, people who receive all their impressions via this center are self-centered crystallized individuals with no apparent emotional capacity and no intuition. It is not a planned evolutionary step, but a karmic one, which has come about as the result of certain conditions prevailing in the West and one that will need adjustment before the Western world can proceed upon the Path.

I have given you much in this lesson and shall require its absorption before presenting you with the next lesson.

As an assignment, write down as many of your own reactive habits as you can discover and the area of mental substance where you find them.

Notes

_____

_____

_____

_____

_____

_____

_____

_____

_____

_____

_____

_____

_____

_____

_____

_____

_____

Lesson 10

Notes

LESSON 11

The Mental Body And
The Plane Of Mind, Part 3

Characteristics of mental polarization;
The synthesis of the lower mind
into a working unit;
Mental polarization as a requirement
for progress upon the Path;
The inward movement and
alignment with the Soul;
Recapitulation of polarization
and alignment

Lesson 11

I trust now that you think you understand what is meant by the concrete mind, and I find among you a certain wonderment as to why this should be the desired place of polarization for the personality. Let me say first that you do not really understand this aspect of the mental body at all, but that you have glimpsed the three transitory stages of polarization that mark the progress of the shift of the personality from the astral nature to the mental nature. The completion of that shift will be characterized by:

1. A thorough cleansing of the lower mental, eliminating all of the crystallized forms to be found therein, maintaining only those response mechanisms which are necessary to the health of the physical instrument and the steady growth of the consciousness.

2. A thorough cleansing of the next layer of mental substance, eliminating all false standards and values and substituting a strong and sure foundation of basic concepts of truth upon which the consciousness can build its temple.

3. A thorough cleansing of the third or innermost layer of concrete mind substance, rendering it free of all self-imposed limitations, and maintaining its steady acceptance of the light of the Soul. It is here that personalities will be polarized and reoriented to the Soul. Here they will set into motion those disciplines necessary to the rebuilding of their threefold instrument and here that they will observe the activities of their lower bodies.

Before continuing with our study of the other aspects of the mental body, let us consider very carefully what we have

The Soul and Its Instrument

covered in this consideration of the concrete mind.

It is very important that each and every one of you understand this well, for it constitutes a part of the training that is imperative to your continued steady growth.

First, I would have you realize that you are a representative of each of the three stages of mental polarization that I have listed in Lesson 10. Each of you has a part of your consciousness held in each of the three layers of concrete mind substance and this is why you are receiving these lessons. If you were completely polarized in any one of the three you would profit nothing from the lessons. To effect the mental polarization explained at the beginning of this lesson, the three layers must be bridged and eventually synthesized into a working unit. This means, then, that each of you:

1. Reacts at times from the lower or outer layer of mind substance, which is neither purely mental nor purely astral. This also means that you are given to irrational conduct at times and in this area you are mastered by your environment.

2. Reacts at times from the second layer of mind substance, which is more mental and given to rationalizing. Here the aspirant doubts, argues, procrastinates, builds illusions and takes exception to.

3. Reacts at times from the third or innermost layer of concrete mind substance, which is characterized by its pairs of opposites. Here aspirants receive realization, are aware of their lacks, practice their first meditations, deliberately commit what they know is wrong action, and here they think they are intelligent. Here it is that they separate on one hand and include on the other. Here they are attempting to establish themselves and here they look to the Soul. Their cry is often,

Lesson 11

"Oh, God, there you are!" for all is beautiful and
"Oh, God, where are you?" for all is lost.

When the personality consciousness is finally polarized
in the innermost layer, and all three layers are integrated into a working unit, the heart and throat centers
will be coordinated and all activity will be impulsed via
the mental polarization from the heart. This means
simply that people who are withdrawn from the outer
world of impressions do not react to circumstances according to the old habit patterns of thought, but rather
operate from the heart of their being, from their true
self. Such people can "turn the other cheek", can forgive
their brothers and love all that breathes, for they are not
inhibited from expression by prejudice and intolerance.

When the heart and throat centers function in perfect
unity, the Light of Intuition breaks through. These people know, but do not know how they know.

This mental integration and perfect balance is brought
about by conscious alignment and reorientation.

By now each one of you knows (if you stop and reflect),
that all activity is the expression of certain energies in
manifestation. Incarnating entities either consciously
wield the energies flowing through them according to a
purpose and plan, or unconsciously react to the impact
upon their automatic response mechanism. The former
stage is that of Discipleship and has been called the
Path of Initiation; the latter stage is that of the purely
human consciousness and has been called the Path of Experience. The shift from the one stage to the other is not
made all at once, but is made in ordered successive
steps according to the overall evolutionary plan and the
initiatory activity of the aspirant. It is aspirants who
must initiate their own growth as they respond to the
evolutionary urge within. I would have you ponder the
last statement as it is one of vital importance to you.

The Soul and Its Instrument

This initiatory activity of aspirants is characterized by the conscious alignment and reorientation referred to above. Until they have done this themselves, they cannot hope to progress upon the Path.

In an earlier lesson I spoke of alignment. I shall do so again in order to focus your attention upon the needed work.

Alignment is the establishment of a path of least resistance for the energies flowing between two given points Let us now consider the two points, and the desired path of least resistance.

The source of energy we recognize, in this instance, as being the Soul. Later it will be necessary to revise and expand this concept in order to include that which is specific. Now we are using the term "Soul" in a general manner as the source of all inflowing energies.

The destination of the energies we recognize as the physical plane of appearances. This, too, will have to be revised and expanded as your comprehension is capable of more understanding.

These energies reach their destination, in this instance, via the etheric network and its system of centers. They are either consciously directed into some form of expression as the entity becomes aware of them in their brain consciousness, or take expression according to the impact upon their automatic response mechanism.

I should also like to point out that many of the energies simply pass through the system with little or no apparent expression. They are of such a high vibratory frequency that they do not impinge upon the consciousness, and any effect is of such a subtle nature, and often so long-ranged, as to be unobserved by the incarnating entity. There are many such energies that the initiate gradually learns to wield for the betterment of humanity.

Lesson 11

The aspirant establishes the alignment for the expression of the energies in the following manner:

1. They withdraw their consciousness, insofar as they are capable, into the innermost layer of concrete mind substance. This will place them in the region of the pituitary gland (the seat of the personality consciousness). Here they observe rather than react. Gradually they detach themselves from the magnetic attraction of the world of impressions and appearances and allow themselves to be attracted to the Life of the Soul. This will accomplish, among others, two important redirections of energy.

   a. The energy of Life itself will be contacted in the brain via the heart center and eventually its secret will be unfolded to the conscious awareness.

   b. The energy that we call creative intelligence will be contacted in the brain via the throat center and eventually its secret will be unfolded to the conscious awareness.

Formerly these two energies entered the system via:

   a. The heart and were instantly channeled into the affairs and activities of the entity via the solar plexus center and the astral vehicle, as reactive expression. It gave life to all of its activities, but without its conscious direction.

   b. The throat and were instantly passed into the affairs and activities of the entity via the sacral center and the astral vehicle as reactive expression. It gave substance (form) to its activities, but without its conscious direction.

The Soul and Its Instrument

2. They throw out a line, as it were, to their Soul, via the ajna center. This line constitutes their attention and forms a bridge between themselves and the abstract plane of mind where their Soul can be contacted.

When the line is firmly established in the ajna center (when the attention becomes fixed), the consciousness is magnetically attracted into the center and the final polarization is complete. The personality consciousness then resides in that area of mind where abstractions take concrete form. They are no longer polarized in the concrete mind aspect of their mental body, neither are they polarized in the abstract aspect of their mental vehicle; but rather they are stationed outside both in the etheric body where the two planes of mind can be viewed and utilized with equal dexterity.

From here the bridging continues; this time between the ajna center and the head center. The flow of energies between the two creates a magnetic field of mind, which is neither abstract nor concrete, but a combination of the two. When this field is sufficiently magnetic, the consciousness of the personality and the consciousness of the Soul are blended into one.

I shall now recapitulate this process of polarization via alignment for your greater understanding.

The polarization in this instance means the vehicle in which the consciousness lives and from which it directs its activities.

Average people are polarized in their astral body. Their alignment with their environment is through the solar plexus center sensory apparatus. They are emotional in nature.

The average aspirant has aligned the solar plexus center

122

with the heart. They are polarized in the astral body. They are aligned with their environment via the solar plexus center, the heart center and the sensory system. They are devotional in nature.

Aspirants verging on Discipleship have aligned their heart center with their throat and are becoming mentally polarized. Their alignment with their environment is via the solar plexus center, the heart center, throat center and their sensory apparatus. They are aspirational in nature.

The Disciple has raised the energies of the solar plexus center to the heart and no longer utilizes the solar plexus as a main center of contact. They have aligned the throat center with the ajna. They are polarized in the etheric and mental body. Their alignment with their environment is via the heart center, throat center, ajna center and sensory apparatus. They are intuitional in nature.

The Initiate has aligned the ajna center with the head center. They are polarized in the light of the Soul. Their alignment with their environment is via the heart, throat, ajna, head and sensory apparatus. They are inspirational in nature.

As an assignment, please explain as nearly as possible, in your own words, your alignment and polarization.

Notes

Lesson 11

Notes

LESSON 12

The Creative Process And
The Rebuilding Of The Persona

The Focus of the Aspirant in the Ajna,
Acting "as if"
The Cave as the Blending
of Will and Wisdom,
How Creativity is Utilized
Through the Meditation Process,
A Meditation Form for
the Manifestation of
the Soul Oriented Persona

Lesson 12

In our last lesson I stated that, "Aspirants initiate their own progress via alignment and re-orientation."

The highest point of alignment constitutes their goal of attainment at any given time. In other words, when they have fastened their attention to the ajna center, it becomes their immediate desired polarization.

The next step which is re-orientation, consists of proceeding "as if." This is one of the most important Laws of the Path for it actually constitutes Initiation. Initiation is a new beginning. Aspirants make a new beginning by acting as if they were polarized in the ajna, as if they were Disciples. This explains the necessity of self-imposed discipline.

Aspirants must then grasp the meaning of Discipleship to the best of their ability and proceed to realize that meaning in action.

In their daily meditations they project their attention into the ajna center, and proceed as if their consciousness was polarized in the head. This cave is actually a cavity in the brain and is the area in which the Soul reflects Its light. It is here that the interplay of energies between the ajna and head centers creates the magnetic field of mind in which the consciousness of Soul and personality are blended.

Disciples meditating in the ajna contact the light of Pure Reason, or the Wisdom aspect of the 2nd Ray via the ajna center. They contact the Plan or Will aspect of the 1st Ray via the head center. As they contact the Plan, the light of Pure Reason gives them understanding or comprehension of it and it then becomes their will or intent, their purpose for incarnation.

The Soul and Its Instrument

After the Plan is contacted and somewhat comprehended, the meditation continues, but this time with a
difference. Though their line of contact with the head
center is maintained, the attention is re-focused onto
the concrete plane of mind via the throat center. Here
the intelligence aspect of the 3rd Ray is contacted and substance is given to their concept of the Plan. It takes form in
mental substance. Remember, the line of contact with
the head center is held intact while the attention is re-
focused into the concrete mind. This is accomplished by the
steady contemplation of the purpose of the form being
created in mental substance. It is the action of will upon
intelligence that produces the form building activity
followed by the vitalization of said form via the power
aspect of the 1st Ray.

Let us recapitulate for just a moment.

Disciples are polarized in the etheric ajna center. They
align with the Plan via the head center and as they receive said Plan in their consciousness, polarized in the
ajna, it is comprehended in abstract form.

Maintaining their stability (polarization in ajna) they
turn their attention to the concrete mind via the throat
and steadily contemplate the purpose or Divine Plan.
Thus Divine Will acts upon intelligence and the abstraction is given concrete form. The head, ajna and
throat centers are functioning together.

The next step in their meditation process is the projection of the completed form into astral substance via its
steady visualization and the spoken word. When the
form can be seen to be completed it is spoken into astral
existence. The word or formula must be ascertained by
the Disciples themselves.

The heart center comes into play at this stage of the
meditation, giving life to the form. The Love aspect of

the 2nd Ray is contacted in the heart and expressed as aspiration. The spoken word then constitutes the manifested aspiration of the Disciples to serve. It is this aspiration that attracts the form into physical plane manifestation. Their love is so great as to give life to their created form.

This brings us right back again to the motive. The Disciples are impulsed to build the form out of a selfless aspiration to serve rather than from a selfish desire to gain. Their spoken word expresses this great love and aspiration and so is creative. The word is made flesh.

In this stage the third eye (related to the ajna center), throat and heart centers are functioning together.

After the form has been given separate astral existence via the spoken word, the Disciples release it from their consciousness knowing full well that their creation will take material form and accepting all karmic obligation for it.

In the above paragraphs I have given you the process for manifestation. Never before have I projected with such clarity this process in written form, because neither humanity nor the Disciples in the world were ready for it. It may seem to you that this is a somewhat dangerous step. It is, but not in the sense you may think. It cannot be utilized without right motive and is, therefore, useless to the misinformed and the unscrupulous. The danger lies in the fact that with increased knowledge comes increased responsibility, and where that responsibility is not shouldered, grave consequences ensue. In this instance the karmic consequences of releasing information fall upon myself, as well as upon those of you who receive it. Our responsibilities must be met if humanity is to benefit from this act of yours and mine.

The aspirants, in proceeding as if they were disciples,

The Soul and Its Instrument

follow this meditation process but with one difference; while they are motivated by the aspiration to serve, their immediate goal is the rebuilding of their threefold personality into a perfected instrument of service. That is the desired immediate manifestation.

This can be accomplished in a number of ways. I am going to give you a form to follow and suggest that it be utilized as a daily individual meditation, after the group meditation is completed.

1. Quickly align the three lower bodies and focus the consciousness in the ajna center.

   Visualize a line of light extending through the cave to the head center.

2. Contact the Divine Plan; in this instance, the planned perfected instrument.

   Using the "I" as the reflected appearance of an essential reality, resolve it back to its reality. Repeat "I" a few times, contemplating it as a concept. Then relax the word form and become receptive to realization.

3. Building the form.

   When realization is grasped, throw out another line. Visualize a line of light extending to the throat center in the spine. Steadily contemplate the purpose and goal of the work, as you watch your abstraction take form.

   This involves:

   a. Stability. The consciousness must be maintained in the ajna center.

b. The abstraction must be allowed to take form. The consciousness does not interfere with the work by attempting to build the form himself. If the realization is held steadily in the ajna and contemplated, along with its purpose and goal, (much easier than it sounds) it will build its own form. This is extremely important.

Now, because you are not yet adept, I must issue a warning at this point, as well as rules that must be followed if you are to steer clear of trouble.

Do not, under any circumstances, attempt to build a picture of a physical form. Believe me, my brothers, you are not adequately equipped to receive as yet such a picture free from glamour. If such a thing should occur, realize it is the result of an impingement of emotion, desire or ambition and discard it as such. Your forms, if the meditation is rightly and honestly motivated, will consist of those disciplines necessary for you to impose upon yourself for the sake of progress.

Before using this meditation, eliminate all preconceived ideas as to what will constitute the realization to be received. Then make sure of your motive. Cast out all desire and all ambition; for if that is the impulse motivating the meditation, it will avail you nothing but trouble. Do not use this meditation if it is wrongly motivated. To continue:

4. The alignment of the consciousness focused in the ajna must be maintained with the head center via the cave, and the throat center.

5. Projection of the form.

When the form is seen as complete (abstraction realized in concrete form), it is visualized in the cave. It may be

The Soul and Its Instrument

seen just in front of the etheric ajna, but that is a reflection. The visualization actually takes place in the cave. The consciousness remains in the ajna, but watches the cave.

The line is then seen as extending down into the heart center in the spine. Disciples in the ajna contemplate their great love for humanity and when the realization of that love reaches its zenith, they sound the audible Om, placing, as it were, their created form on the Om. Remember, the Om carries the expression of their selfless love.

6. Release of form.

Then speak the words,

"So it is in Divine Law and Order"

and take your mind from the work done.

Lesson 12

Notes

The Soul and Its Instrument

Notes

Lesson 12

Notes

LESSON 13

The Body Of Knowledge
And Energies From Past Lives, Part 1

The Problem of Identity,
The Purpose of Experience,
The Goal of Unity

Lesson 13

We come now to that part of the instrument that is somewhat difficult to consider because of the glamour attached to the subject. I am speaking anent the body of knowledge and the energies accumulated over many past incarnations. This subject, around which so much glamour has been built, must be clarified, for the past does constitute a part of the instrument through which the Soul must work in its service to the Plan.

I have not previously brought this subject into the Light in the manner that I am now undertaking, for there were not enough conscious Disciples in the world who could be depended upon to hold it in that Light. This condition has been somewhat changed and today I find those Disciples who can, if they so choose, act as custodians of certain information to be released to others later as time and right opportunity permit.

As I release this information, I do so with the prayer that all who receive it will consciously lend their efforts to pierce the glamour of the past and so bring about an adjustment of Karma within the human family.

Certain questions have been and should continue to be posed by so-called thinkers everywhere, if the darkness of ignorance is to lose its power over the human family. Some of these questions are:

1. What is my identity? Who am I actually? This question inevitably brings into the awareness of thinkers the fact that they are self-conscious entities persisting throughout eternity. They cannot contemplate their own identities without realizing their essential Divinity; the fact that they are eternal (for it is impossible to actually conceive of not being), and the fact that all other

people are as they themselves are; therefore, all people are their brothers.

At the same time, they come to realize that which they are *not*. They are not their physical body, nor their emotions, nor even their thoughts. They recognize them as energies they have appropriated and put to use for a purpose. The purpose they recognize as being experience, and in this manner they begin to separate themselves from the experiences they have undertaken. They no longer identify their experiences as themselves, but gradually disentangle themselves from the web of illusion that has held them prisoner for so long.

They are not personalities.

They are neither men nor women, male nor female.

They are not a king, queen, husband, wife, shoe salesperson, business executive, etc.

They are not wealthy, poor, smart, stupid, ill, etc.

They *are* the Soul, conscious of themselves as such, and of the role they are presently playing. Their personality, their bodies, their status in life, etc., they recognize as being a part of their experience, and as such, separate and apart from themselves. This brings them to the second question.

> 2. What is the purpose of all this experience? If they are not really the personality nor the vehicles of manifestation, then what is the purpose of these vehicles?

The first answer they arrive at is the evolution of consciousness. That must be the reason; but then again they become bewildered. If they, as the Soul, are capable of creating these conditions, it must have been done

142

Lesson 13

with a knowledge of what it would lead to. If that is so, the very fact of creation presupposes an evolution of consciousness far in advance of anything they can even imagine as a goal.

This line of questioning finally brings the realization that each experience they have known has been but a phase in the process of building an instrument of contact, suited for some definite purpose. Hidden within the depths of the consciousness is the objective for which they are sacrificing so much, and they know without a doubt, that evolution of consciousness alone is not the answer, but only partial, in that it, too, is brought about with a larger purpose in mind.

Now their mind strains to find the answer, to become aware of that larger purpose, and because their realization of identity is not complete, but an expanding awareness of reality, the answer comes to them in degrees.

They are building an instrument through which they can carry out a definite objective.

This building process has been going on over a long period of incarnations, and will continue for how many more, they cannot imagine.

Because of the nature of the vehicles they now inhabit, they realize that the final one will be a super instrument of contact with the plane of existence upon which it is being created.

Because they themselves have undertaken to imprison themselves in form, or substance, and are in a process of liberation from that form, they realize that the objective is the final liberation of all consciousness from form.

They involute into matter or substance; vivify and stimulate the inherent consciousness of substance itself

The Soul and Its Instrument

to awareness, and with it, evolve to liberation from form. Thus is the marriage of Spirit to Matter, and the consequent birth of the Son revealed.

They, as pure Spirit, merged with substance, and as the consciousness of both, are returning home.

Beyond that, humanity's present comprehension cannot go. This much, however, does give them a realization of purpose, great enough to enable them to grasp the concept of Service.

Within each atom of substance is locked a unit of consciousness. As the Spirit appropriates substance and takes it on as form, It is blending with that imprisoned consciousness. Its merging stimulates the consciousness to self-awareness, and thus the liberated Soul is born.

Meditation upon this will bring a greater realization of Christ's words, "I and My Father are One."

We see, then, that all vehicles appropriated in past incarnations are in truth one vehicle that is in a process of construction. Each incarnation was but a step in the building process; each vehicle but a building block in the greater Temple.

To ones who create, the ones who in meditation observe the carrying out of their purpose, the building blocks are not separated by time and space. To them there is no time nor space, but only the vast manifestation of the Plan.

Realize now that you are *not* your experiences. You are *not* a personality, but rather an entity that is utilizing that personality as an instrument of contact with consciousness. Each experience is a part of that instrument, and when regarded as such, becomes an opportunity for service to the Plan itself.

Lesson 13

I have given you much in this lesson upon which to meditate. I shall allow you time to receive and absorb the realization underlying the words before continuing. I would advise you to contemplate deeply the meaning contained in the lesson, before you go on to the next one. Ask yourself the questions posed on these pages and write your own answers. Hand the paper in to your teacher before proceeding with the next lesson.

Notes

Lesson 13

Notes

LESSON 14

The Body Of Knowledge
And Energies From Past Lives, Part 2

The past as an instrument of
the Soul, Causal Body, Egoic Egg;
The Monad, Consciousness and
the three permanent atoms;
The redemption of consciousness
identified with form;
Past lives and the identification
with experience;
The United States and Atlantis:
the karmic obligation of a group Soul;
The glamours of the past;
Karmic relationships between individuals;
Karmic relationships within a group;
The application of Divine Love
to initiate right relationship

Lesson 14

The past is a part of the instrument through which the Soul must work. It is actually a series of building blocks which are being utilized in the construction of the super instrument of contact. This instrument is called the "Causal Body" or "Egoic Egg". It is spheroidal in shape, as are all bodies, and expands with each incarnation until it becomes a sphere of pulsating light of great beauty. It is constructed of:

1. A positive central life, that which has been called the "Christ Consciousness".

This is the true Son of God, the projected consciousness of the Monad.

2. Three permanent atoms:

    a. The mental permanent atom

    b. The astral permanent atom

    c. The physical permanent atom

Each of these three permanent atoms is a center of contact with three states of consciousness:

    a. The individual Spiritual Soul

    b. The human Soul

    c. The animal Soul

These three states of consciousness constitute:

    a. That which has blended with Spirit and become Light

151

The Soul and Its Instrument

    b. That which has reached self-awareness and stands beneath the Light

    c. That which is aware of sensation and remains in darkness

When Sons of God incarnate, they project a part of their consciousness into the vehicles that are constructed around and colored by the three permanent atoms. This projected consciousness, which is in reality Divine and Eternal, blends with the form nature and the inherent consciousness within the form, and tends to identify with that of which it has become a part. Thus the awareness loses sight of its real identity and becomes a prisoner to form, bound in the illusion of the personality.

It must be remembered that the projected consciousness does not return to its original plane after each incarnation in physical form. Once it has descended into matter it does not return until it has not only overcome the limitations of the form nature, but has brought the consciousness inherent in the form to its own enlightened state of awareness. Thus when it returns it is as it was in the beginning, plus a new quality or tone derived from the new consciousness, which has been raised from inertia to activity. In other words, the Christ Consciousness descended from its high plane of Light to merge with a state of consciousness that was more or less inert. In that descent, the Christ took on the condition of that with which He merged and as a combined state of the two, is once again returning home.

The evolution of the projected consciousness takes many, many lives. In between those physical incarnations, the Soul resides on the plane determined by its own evolution. It may enter any one of the devachanic worlds according to its belief, or as it realizes its identity it may pass on to the various aspects of the mental plane, into the Master's Ashram, etc. It does not, however, return

Lesson 14

to the Father until it has become a liberated Son of God.

There are certain types of experience that each Soul undertakes before it reaches consciousness of itself as a Soul. One of the glamours attached to the subject of reincarnation is the curiosity individuals will feel, as to who or what they may have been in another body. Those who are particularly unhappy with their present status in life will invariably "remember or recall", to use their words, an incarnation in which they were some great personage. Seldom do you hear of an individual "recalling" a former incarnation in which the individual was nondescript. This has done much to discredit the whole subject, as well as many other ideas voiced by those who have no knowledge whereof they speak.

To offset this type of glamour, I shall here list five classifications of experience into which each one of you who are capable of understanding this teaching and of serving the race in its present condition, must have incarnated during the past ages.

1. The experiences of murder, rape, adultery, prostitution, theft, etc. This type of experience is no longer a necessary part of the manifesting conditions of the incarnating Soul, because the human Soul has evolved beyond the polarization that brought it on. Its persistence is but the cleaning up of Karma and the continuance of a racial habit pattern of thought. Disciples can, in a united effort, throw light upon this condition and release humanity from its hold.

2. The experience of war.

3. The experience of wealth, of poverty, of ruler, of servant or slave, of husband, of wife, of mother, of father, of son, of daughter, etc. This type of experience continues as a necessary manifesting

condition into which the Soul incarnates to achieve awareness of relationship both to things and people.

4. The experience of meditation; an incarnation or more in which the major part of the life was spent in meditation, often as a Priest, Lama, etc.

5. The experience of successful, creative activity.

All of these classifications are experiences that are the natural result of the overall evolution of the Soul. They are conditions through which it has lived, but they are not the Soul itself. To say, "I was a queen", or any other great personage in a past life, is ignorance. Nor would such a statement come from anyone who had achieved integration with their past. They would realize that these experiences have been shared with their brothers and that to have played the role of a queen is no more important than to have played the role of a mother. The importance of any incarnation is only in its relationship to the whole and this should be realized by all disciples.

Another point I should here like to bring out is the fact that the present civilization, particularly that of the United States, is a reincarnation of the Group Soul who formerly incarnated as the Atlantean civilization. This Group Soul brings with it into incarnation a karmic relationship to the world, which is displayed in the activities in which it has engaged since its conception. It comes in during a cyclic period of opportunity in which the possibility of its karmic adjustment is obvious. Its role, in the carrying out of that adjustment, is that of the liberator and the salvager. Its task is the liberation of the Soul from darkness, and the salvaging of all that can be considered good out of our present civilization. It can, if it so chooses, become the peace maker, and bring an end to the ceaseless wars of the past. All of this explains why the Hierarchy is giving so much of its attention to this nation, and why the Truth movement has gained such strength during recent years.

Within the United States, and, of course, other parts of the world, there are many disciples who are becoming aware of the past with its karmic obligation, and the part which they can play in the adjustment of that karma. These are the ones who realize the value of group service and recognize that only through a united group effort can the final adjustments be made. No one person can turn the tide of events from destruction to construction, but the united energies of all disciples of the Christ can bring in the new era in which peace and revelation will be the dominating quality.

Therefore, those of you who sense the necessary work ahead, and those of you who may "recall" something of the past, waste not your energies in a consideration of who and what you may think you were or in attaching importance to that which you have done, may be doing or are preparing to do. Once again, in service there is no competition, only cooperation and love.

The glamours of importance, guilt, fanaticism, revenge (often in the form of violence), and ambition, so completely surround the past that almost any clear thinking anent it is impossible. These glamours blind the perception of students, just as fog will blind the eyes of a person, so that all they see is blurred and out of perspective. All students who detect this in themselves should make it a point to turn the light of the Soul upon the past and allow the Soul to wash away illusion. Do not seek knowledge of former incarnations. Do not speculate with the concrete mind anent these things, but leave them to the Soul to reveal in its own time.

Another point that I should like to bring to your attention at this time is the fact of karmic relationship between brothers; of how it is recognized and adjusted. Remember, the basic relationship between any two individuals is brotherhood. The form that relationship may take in the world of the personality is determined by the inter-related karma which arises from the past, as well as the attitude with which the association is approached. Karmic relationships fall into categories that I shall explain as follows:

1. Physical relationship.

This is the result of past association on the plane of dense substance and controls, to a certain degree the family into which the Soul is born. The relationship of the three permanent atoms to the other permanent atoms will often control the ties of the flesh.

2. Emotional relationship.

This can arise out of past association on the emotional level, where certain ties have been erected and must, as yet, be transcended before the Soul is free to serve without the limitation of emotional relationship; or it may be the result of two individuals coming together for the first time, with a common emotional interest. The latter is then the beginning or initiation of a karmic relationship that will bring the two back into incarnation together again and again until it has been adjusted and all that remains is the Soul tie.

3. Mental relationship.

This relationship is brought about by past mental association or the meeting of minds for a common purpose and is somewhat easier to adjust than the above, for mental ties are not so binding, nor so long lasting as emotional ones.

4. Group relationship.

This is brought about through past association. Groups

Lesson 14

of Souls come in and go out together, and in the process of living they create the conditions into which they are karmically impelled to serve. This type of relationship is completely different from that of any other. The Soul tie is so strong and the realization of a common service karma so great that it will draw these people together against tremendous obstacles arising on the plane of the personality. In spite of personality friction, they will hold together and eventually arrive at an attitude of co-operation based upon mutual love and understanding.

Within the group there are certain karmic relationships that fall into a different classification than the others. These are a source of difficulty until accepted and understood by all members of the group, allowing all individuals to assume their rightful relationship to all other individuals and to the whole. The relationships are determined by a number of things; the particular field of experience in which the Soul has spent the most time, thus achieving abilities along a certain line, as well as making karma that must be adjusted in the course of its service; the Ray makeup of the Soul of the personality, and the consequent training it has undergone in the past; the relative evolution of the incarnating entity and the resultant polarization of the awareness.

The karmic relationships within a group may be listed as follows:

1. The group leader.

This individual will constitute the head center of the group and will provide the 1st Ray drive which will enable the group to accomplish its purpose.

2. The group guardians.

These may be any number of individuals whose experience has provided them with the Wisdom to balance the energies of the leader, which may at times be impulsed without discrimination. These are the disciples who back the leader, who offer counsel to all members of the group without discrimination against another member and who provide the Love Wisdom which holds the group together as a group. They are the heart center of the group.

3. The group public relations center.

These are the disciples who are the main points of contact between the group and the environment in which the group serves. They provide the intelligent activity aspect, in whatever form is necessary, from the group to those outside the group. They are responsible for right relationship between the group and the world, for they bring the fact of the group to the attention of the outer world. They act as the throat center of the group.

4. The group nucleus.

This is the subjective group, consisting of the group leader and a member or members of each of the other group centers. Together they act as the mind of the group, carrying the light of the Soul to the brain. They are the ones who make possible the form through which the activity of group expression can manifest.

When you sense a karmic relationship on the personality plane, or an obstacle to the manifestation of group right relationship, realize that it can be adjusted through an application of Divine Love and the realization of brotherhood. Any relationship other than brotherhood is superficial and at best a substitute for the real thing.

Establish the relationship of brotherhood with all humanity and know peace. Accept the responsibilities arising out of your present relationships, for you have in some way earned them, and with Love in your hearts,

Lesson 14

establish right relationship within your group, your environment and the world of humanity.

PEACE BE UNTO YOU

Notes

Lesson 14

Notes

_____

_____

_____

_____

_____

_____

_____

_____

_____

_____

_____

_____

_____

_____

_____

_____

_____

_____

LESSON 15

The Seven Rays, The Personality, and Evolution, Part 1

The causal body and the cave;
The seven rays and the causal body;
The seven rays defined;
The evolution of the Soul and
its utilization of the seven rays
(with an example of the process);
Considerations of the Soul

Lesson 15

Each permanent atom is an aggregate of all experience that has been undergone on its particular plane. In other words, the essence of an entire incarnation is absorbed into each of the three permanent atoms and is, then, added to all that has gone before.

The causal body or auric egg, as it has been called, contains the reflected consciousness of the Christ; the three permanent atoms and the outer shell or envelope. It is contacted in the center of the head in what has been called the cave, (the brain cavity) just above the pineal gland. As the personality consciousness becomes aware of it, it takes form as the light in the head. The "lighted lamp" is symbolic of this stage of development.

Focused into and through the causal body are the five dominating Rays that constitute the equipment of the Soul; the Ray upon which the Soul is found, the three sub-rays upon which the three vehicles are found, and the sub-ray that constitutes the way of least resistance for the integration of the three-fold personality.

This subject of the Rays is a very large one and while I do not intend this to be a lesson on the Rays, it is necessary that I go into them somewhat in order to clarify my subject.

There are seven types of Ray energy which are the seven expressions of Divinity. These Rays, which pour through the etheric network and its system of centers, constitutes the sum total of energies apportioned by the incarnating entity at any given time, for the purpose of its expression. They enter the system via the causal body and are released into the three vehicles via the three permanent atoms, the etheric network and its centers. For instance, the Ray energy upon which the

165

mental body is found enters the causal body through the Central Life, is focused into and through the mental permanent atom and is released to the mental body via the throat center and the etheric network.

The incarnating entity consciously or unconsciously receives the energy (usually misinterprets its Divine meaning or intended expression) and directs it into those channels that constitute the normal habit pattern of thought. The response the entity makes to the impact of energy upon its awareness and its consequent interpretation, determines the experience to follow.

The seven Ray energies are identified as follows:

1. 1st Ray of Divine Will and Power.
2. 2nd Ray of Divine Love-Wisdom.
3. 3rd Ray of Active Intelligence.
4. 4th Ray of Harmony through Conflict.
5. 5th Ray of Concrete Knowledge and Science.
6. 6th Ray of Devotion to an Ideal.
7. 7th Ray of Ceremonial Magic or Divine Law and Order.

A study of and meditation upon the identification of the Rays will reveal their Divine Intention, making it possible for humanity to become a part of the Universal Divine Expression.

All substance is colored by one or another of these Rays, meaning that it has been impregnated with an intention. It is then released to the Souls awaiting incarnation. The Soul appropriates certain of that substance and builds the form through which it will gain experience. Thus the threefold personality, a conditional state of existence, is constructed and colored so as to attract to itself the desired experiences. As an example I shall draw an hypothetical parallel that will make this more readily understood.

Consider a 2nd Ray Soul in a process of incarnating. It has first to consider the Ray makeup of the last incarnation which was, in this case:

1. Soul Ray — 2nd Ray of Love-Wisdom. That is to say, the way of least resistance was and still is, that of inclusive Love.

2. Personality Ray — 3rd Ray of Active Intelligence. The way of least resistance for the integration of the personality was constant activity, in which dramatization and outer organization played an important part. Its experiences were largely dramatic and had to do with form.

3. Ray of the Mental Body — 5th Ray of Concrete Knowledge and Science. This gave it an analytical mind capable of organization and one-pointed purpose.

4. Ray of the Astral Body — 1st Ray of Will and Power, which gave it a strong dominating emotional body capable of adhering to any realized plan. This one was capable of sacrifice on an emotional level to obtain the heart's desire.

5. Ray of the Physical Body — 6th Ray of Devotion, which gave it fanatical devotion to and need of a physical ideal.

It can be seen that in this incarnation the Soul had little chance of making itself felt, while the personality had a very good opportunity for integration. The polarization was in a process of transition from astral to mental (which was somewhat difficult, due to the power of the

The Soul and Its Instrument

1st Ray astral, and the physical brain recognition of a needed ideal). The ideal took the form of the idealized personality due to the power of the astral, the organization of the mind and the dramatization of the personality. The incarnation was spent in the endeavor to glorify the personality and was quite successful insofar as the awareness of the "I" was concerned.

In this next incarnation, the Soul wishes to continue the shift of polarization from astral to mental and to stabilize it. The Ray makeup in this case will be:

1. Soul Ray — 2nd Ray of Love-Wisdom.
2. Personality Ray — 3rd Ray of Active Intelligence (again).
3. Mental Ray — 1st Ray of Will and Power (transfer from astral to mental).
4. Astral Ray — 6th Ray of Devotion, (transfer from physical to astral).
5. Physical Ray — 7th Ray of Ceremony, or Law and Order.

Once again, this integrating Ray is that of Active Intelligence, and this time the personality is more wise in its interpretation of its meaning. The 1st Ray of power has shifted to the mental body, giving it more strength and endurance. The 6th Ray has shifted to the astral body, bringing the ideal into the emotional nature and providing a path of least resistance for the expression of the 2nd Ray Soul. The ideal will still concern the glorified personality, but it will have become an emotional drive for power. The 2nd Ray Soul will bring conflict to the personality by its release of Love into the astral body (which will be interpreted as love on the emotional level). The love of individuals will be in conflict with the drive for power. The head will rule, but the heart will suffer, thus certain karma made in the last incarnation

Lesson 15

will be balanced, as well as new karma initiated.

The 7th Ray physical will aid the personality in its ability to establish order and the end of the incarnation will see a partial mental polarization, an emotional awareness of love and a greater integration of the threefold personality.

In the next incarnation this same 2nd Ray Soul will utilize a:

1. 6th Ray personality.

2. 1st Ray mental.

3. 4th Ray astral.

4. 7th Ray physical.

The mind will become aware of higher purpose; the astral aware of conflict to a greater degree than heretofore; the physical still capable of order, but a battleground for the battle between the mind and the emotions. The personality will be torn between its devotion to a realized higher self (Soul) and its devotion to loved ones.

This one will near the path as a probationer, realize mental polarization and bring certain disciplines to bear upon the emotional nature.

It can be seen, then, that the Soul awaiting incarnation, must consider the following, in the light of the development of the incarnating consciousness:

1. The former incarnation; its polarization and degree of integration; its Ray makeup; consequent experience; and resultant karma.

The Soul and Its Instrument

2. The desired polarization and desired degree of integration; the necessary experience and the karma to be precipitated; and the consequent choice of Rays.

3. Its realization of the Divine Plan and the way of least resistance for Its manifestation.

When the incarnating consciousness has become aware of Divine Purpose to the extent that it has become an aspirant, it begins to cooperate with the Soul by an intelligent direction of its Ray energy into manifested expression. It endeavors to aid by consciously shifting the polarization onto the mental plane and by orienting to the life of the Soul.

At a certain stage in this development, the disciple is taught to utilize the past in service. I shall go into this in the next lesson. In the meantime, contemplate the meaning of the 7 Rays and write your understanding of their Divine Intention. Hand the paper in to your teacher before proceeding with the next lesson.

Lesson 15

Notes

_____

_____

_____

_____

_____

_____

_____

_____

_____

_____

_____

_____

_____

_____

_____

Notes

Lesson 15

Notes

LESSON 16

Difficulties And Solutions
To Problems On The Path

Confusion as the aspirant
evolves into the disciple;
Difficulties are left-overs from the past;
Opposition from loved ones;
Transmutation, love and re-orientation
to soul rather than personality;
The wisdom available from the past;
The recognition of patterns
and habits from the past;
Integration with the past

Lesson 16

We are now concerned with the personality conscious-ness who has become aware of the Soul, is endeavoring to live as a disciple and has realized the need for Soul control of the threefold instrument.

It goes without saying that they are rightly motivated and are dedicated to service. They are often perplexed, however, and frustrated in their honest desire to serve. They have realized the Plan to a degree and in attempt-ing to serve that Plan, meet with obstacles on every hand; the opposition of loved ones, circumstances that demand their time and attention and often difficult and unruly personalities.

This is only natural and a normal condition for all disci-ples at this stage of the Path. Actually, they are still more aspirants than disciples, for they have not yet learned how to shoulder the cross and follow the Christ.

Those of you who find yourselves in this state, stop feel-ing different, and realize that it, too, is but a transient experience. It will pass to take its relative place in the whole. That passing can be more quickly achieved by an intelligent observation of the situation, and applied Wisdom.

In the first place, the obstacles they recognize are all left-overs from the past and can be transcended. Not only can they be transcended, but they can be utilized as stepping stones upon the Path to full Soul conscious-ness. Remember, the Path is found within in medita-tion. Disciples become the Path as they manifest it out-wardly. Think on this. It is important.

The opposition of loved ones to their desire for service is very common and is brought on always by the karma

The Soul and Its Instrument

between the two and the disciples themselves. Individuals, particularly husbands, wives, children, close friends, etc., who claim a close personality tie with disciples and who demand their attention are right in their demand. This is the first thing disciples must face. Service does not mean the dropping of one responsibility for another, but rather the recognition of the present responsibility and the additional burden of more responsibility. Until the present burden is recognized, accepted and met, true service is not possible. I would have you think on this, for all over the world today we find a deplorable condition present; would-be disciples building great glamour anent service, leaving their rightful places and responsibilities to others and going out into the world (so to speak) to serve.

The answer, in this case, is to accept your present responsibility as earned karmic obligation. Transmute your resentments into Divine Love and allow It to sweep through the astral nature and into the environment. Apply the Truth and the realized concepts of service to those who have claim upon your time and attention, working with as much love and zeal as you would if doing that which appears to you as the more desirable.

At the same time, detach from these persons as a personality and think of them as Souls with all humanity. Love them, but no more than any other, and out of that love, serve humanity through them. Remember that in serving the few, the many are served for are not all inter-related and inter-dependent?

When you have achieved an inner realization of the Soul tie, rather than ties of the personality, and have achieved the ability to establish right relationship in your environment, all opposition will disappear naturally and without harm to any person.

The situations that demand time and attention are the disciple's own making. Clear thinking, love and application

Lesson 16

of Truth will change them from obstacles to opportunities for service.

The unruly personality is a result of the past. Many lifetimes of a misdirection of Divine Energy establishes habits difficult to break.

Disciples should first discover their Ray makeup. This they do by a meditation upon the intended expression of the Rays and an intelligent observation of their own tendencies. They should observe the activities of the three vehicles and their effect upon the sphere of influence.

What effect do their thoughts have upon themselves and others?

Of what type are their thought patterns and what Ray do these seem to express? Is this expression a positive or a negative one?

Carry this same observation to the other aspects of the personality.

The next step for disciples is the discovery of that Wisdom that has been carried over, but is apparently dormant. They must be extremely careful in this activity so as not to awaken that which is definitely undesirable, such as ancient habits which the race no longer has need of.

They realize first that in past incarnations they, as Soul have achieved Wisdom anent situations similar to those which they now meet. This is not the first time they have undergone certain experiences, but often these are repeated again and again out of habit. If they could but realize it, the answers to many of their problems lie in the consciousness of the Soul. Very often karma is relived over and over when it could be transcended through Wisdom.

The Soul and Its Instrument

Consider first the problems which have continually repeated in this incarnation, for they are most likely the repeaters of long standing. Stop reacting and take them into meditation, realizing that you are placing them in the light of the Soul. Cease trying to formulate an answer with the concrete mind and utilize it as a receiving station for illumination.

In this manner you will recover much apparently lost (though only untapped) Wisdom and so become integrated with the past. This does not mean you will arrive at memory of the past, nor is that desired. It does mean that you will be expanding your awareness and so utilizing that part of the instrument in service. Thus you will have made another step in progress and stepped up the efficiency of your instrument.

As an assignment, please write what you consider as constituting your Ray makeup and give your reason for that conclusion.

Lesson 16

Notes

The Soul and Its Instrument

Notes

Lesson 16

Notes

_____

_____

_____

_____

_____

_____

_____

_____

_____

_____

_____

_____

_____

_____

_____

_____

_____

184

LESSON 17

The Seven Rays, The Personality, And Evolution, Part 2

Recapitulation of the evolution
of the personality (using example
of personality lives from Lesson 15);
Explanation of future growth
and the coming age of the seventh ray;
A group process for ray determination

Lesson 17

In Lesson 15 I explained how the threefold personality is constructed and colored so as to attract to itself the needed experiences. In that lesson I also drew an hypothetical parallel in order to clarify the subject.

In this lesson I shall do the same thing, but from a different perspective. We shall consider the construction of a threefold vehicle by the Soul whose projected consciousness has arrived at an awareness of purpose and is therefore consciously cooperating somewhat with the Soul.

The consciousness in the first incarnation to be considered has entered the Path as a probationer, has become aware of the Soul and has realized mental polarization. It is still engaged in the battle between the pairs of opposites. In this incarnation its Ray makeup was:

1. Soul Ray of Love-Wisdom
2. Personality Ray of Active Intelligence
3. Mental Ray of Concrete Knowledge and Science
4. Astral Ray of Power
5. Physical Ray of Devotion

Because of its point in evolution, the consciousness was vaguely aware of its Soul purpose and the way of inclusive love. This brought conflict to bear, in that its mind knew love of scientific knowledge, its astral body knew love of power and its physical brain recognized science as the ideal. God and religion were scorned, yet this person's mind could not escape the realization of a higher intelligence than that of the brain. The concept of service spurred this person on in scientific investigation, which increased this person's lack of faith in orthodox religion, attempts to find a concrete answer to life

The Soul and Its Instrument

and a reluctant belief in what this person called a supreme or guiding intelligence. The person made many emotional sacrifices to prove that humanity's brain was the only reality, but only proved conclusively that it was but an instrument for use by some higher, more intelligent being. Thus, this person entered the Path as a probationer.

In the second incarnation to be considered, this same Soul is utilizing the following equipment:

1. 2nd Ray Soul
2. Personality Ray of Active Intelligence
3. Mental Ray of Power (transfer from astral)
4. Astral Ray of Devotion (transfer from Physical)
5. Physical Ray of Ceremony, or Law and Order

The individual comes in this time with a background of unrealized scientific knowledge and is, therefore, naturally drawn to scientific education. The 1st Ray of Power gives a clear purposeful mind with great endurance and a recognition very early of the Soul.

The Ray of Devotion gives an emotional longing for and devotion to the Soul and thus this person becomes an aspirant.

The Ray of Ceremony or Law and Order gives a physical vehicle capable of organization and drive. This same Ray colors the brain cells in such a way that they grasp and reflect Soul purpose and therefore swing the personality consciousness into a greater awareness of the inner reality.

The Ray of Active Intelligence accents form, which provides the conflict between the pairs of opposites; Soul and form, form and Soul.

Lesson 17

This one unconsciously begins real service in this incarnation, that of bringing abstraction into concrete form. This person adjusts much karma and so suffers, but realization of purpose, steadily integrating consciousness and aspiration, are preparing this individual for discipleship.

In the next incarnation, this same Soul will utilize the following equipment:

1. 2nd Ray Soul

2. Personality Ray of Devotion

3. Mental Ray of Power

4. Astral Ray of Harmony

5. Physical Ray of Ceremony, or Law and Order

Slowly the Soul is preparing the projected consciousness for a 2nd Ray personality and service on the Teaching Ray. Devotion to an ideal has become the integrating Ray of the threefold personality, and the ideal is already well established as the Soul or Higher Self and the way of inclusive Love.

The astral body has swung on to the 4th Ray of Harmony through Conflict and the real battle between Soul and personality begins. The renunciation makes itself known to the consciousness as the necessary discipline and the question of motive enters the awareness.

The astral nature puts up a last ditch fight to regain its supremacy in the life and affairs of the incarnating entity. Because of its great strength, gained earlier on the 1st Ray of Power, the battle is severe. The mental polarization, with its 1st Ray Power, is the stronger, however, and will establish once and for all its control over the emotions. The battle between Soul and personality will then shift its focus to the mental plane.

189

The Soul and Its Instrument

The aspirant will need to beware of a mental tendency to superiority, pride and a drive for power. Herein lies danger and choice.

The 7th Ray will give this individual, in this incarnation, much physical magnetism, an intuitive understanding of law and an ability to work with form to advantage.

This incarnation offers great opportunity for progress. Its finish will see the incarnating entity well established on either the right or the left hand path, depending upon its own choice.

This same equipment, if utilized by a Soul whose projected consciousness had realized discipleship, would be handled somewhat differently:

1. The Soul Ray of Love-Wisdom would indicate teaching as the field of service and the disciple would establish as a teacher of the Ancient Wisdom.

2. The Personality Ray of Devotion would indicate some crystallization in regard to Truth, usually gained during some former incarnation of devotion to a sensed but unrealized, and, therefore, distorted ideal; a karmic tie and therefore obligation to the Master Jesus and Christianity; and the church (usually Catholic), as at least one area of service karma. In other words, while this one would be a teacher of Ancient Wisdom, service karma would bring this one into the area of the church. This one's service, then, would be to concentrate upon the uniting or synthesizing of the Eastern and Western philosophies; for the other aspect of karma (that of the 2nd Ray Soul) would obligate this one to the East and, therefore, the Buddha. This individual's greater

Lesson 17

service, then, would be the bringing of peace to the disciples of both the Buddha and the Christ.

3. The Mental Ray of Power would give this individual a good control of the two lower vehicles, but provide this individual with conflict. The 1st Ray tends to isolate, and when predominant in the mental body, is often separative. The disciple would necessarily have to detach from the personality, and will to Love.

4. The 4th Ray of Harmony through Conflict would provide the Soul with an astral vehicle capable of transmutation and conflict would be transmuted into harmony. This would give this one the intuitive understanding necessary to work with the Eastern and Western doctrines.

5. The 7th Ray of Ceremony would indicate again a karmic obligation to either the Catholic Church or the Masonic movement and would allow the disciple to work successfully with ritual and mantric form.

Why have I gone into such detail in Lesson 15, and in this lesson, when you apparently have such little background for understanding? The question has two answers, which I shall explain as follows:

With the coming in of the 7th Ray of Law and Order at this time, much knowledge anent the Rays is overshadowing humanity. It is possible for groups of dedicated disciples to be impressed by this knowledge, and hence, to aid their own growth by an intelligent understanding of their own Ray makeup. All individuals have their own peculiar problems arising out of their peculiar Ray makeup, and their past experiences. An understanding of their problems will render them more capable of fitting themselves for service, as well as providing them

The Soul and Its Instrument

with the Light to shine upon the Path for their brothers.

When I tell you that it is possible for groups of dedicated disciples to be impressed by the knowledge of the Rays, I do not mean that they will receive communication from an entity or groups of entities. The Knowledge overshadows humanity and can be intuited by those who can tune in on the right mental frequency. Right motive, a sincere love of humanity and meditation makes this possible.

I am presenting you with an assignment that will, if accepted, take as many weeks as there are members of your group and possibly more. The assignment is optional and is to be voted upon. Its acceptance must be unanimous, if at all, and for that reason, I shall ask you to consider it very carefully before a vote is taken. The assignment is as follows:

One member of the group will volunteer each week as a subject of study by the other members of the group. They will study the person in the following manner:

1. Attempt to arrive at the individual's Ray makeup.

2. Discover whether or not it is directed according to its Divine Intention.

3. Discover the individual's particular problem and in what body it is focused.

4. Discover how best the problem can be solved.

They will work as a group, not as individuals, and together will write up a case record of the person under observation, which is to be given to their teacher at the end of each study.

The member under observation will not take part in the

Lesson 17

group activity, except as an object of study.

If this assignment is carried out, it will be absolutely necessary for each member of the group to detach from the personality and personalities. There will be no further lessons until the assignment is either rejected immediately, or carried out to its completion.

I realize that this is a difficult assignment and a test of the group; therefore, I leave you free to make your own choice.

PEACE BE UNTO YOU.

Notes

_____

_____

_____

_____

_____

_____

_____

_____

_____

_____

_____

_____

_____

_____

_____

_____

_____

Lesson 17

Notes

_____

_____

_____

_____

_____

_____

_____

_____

_____

_____

_____

_____

_____

_____

_____

_____

LESSON 18

The Condition Of The Personality
And Past Actions

Acceptance of the Disciple's
present instrument;
Attitude concerning personality problems;
Reasons difficulties are present;
Present difficulties as service;
Healing accomplished through right attitude

Lesson 18

We know now that we have a threefold instrument of contact with the world in which we live and we know also that it is through this instrument that we are obliged to serve.

I would say that disciples must not only fit their instrument for service, but that this is done by making right use of that which they already have through some type of service activity. Our equipment, whatever it might be, is karmic, in that until we have used it to the best advantage, we cannot exchange it for better. It would be wise for student disciples to give this serious thought. For even should they discarnate, and thus shed the defects of their physical vehicles, they would be forced back, under Law, into like vehicles, when again their cycle of incarnation brought them into appearance.

We find a condition of procrastination, and at times, even apathy, among aspirants and would-be disciples, due to the type of equipment with which they are forced to work. Often they sit back, entering not into service because of some handicap that renders them immobile. There is the common belief among them that later (when they are better equipped), they will take their places among the hard workers of the race. My brothers, this is not so, for aspirants or disciples will not be better equipped until they have utilized that which they have for the betterment of their brothers.

It is then up to the incarnating consciousness to put its threefold instrument into right use and thereby free itself of that which serves as a handicap. Think on this, for there is among you much distortion anent this subject. All of you, and I say "all" with deliberate intent, are handicapped in some manner, in one, or more often, all three of the instruments.

The Soul and Its Instrument

Some disciples are forced to function through instruments that are more of a handicap than those of their brothers, such as the physically deformed, maimed, crippled, blind, deaf, etc. Many carry the burden of long, drawn out illnesses, pain, etc., but all share this condition to a greater or lesser degree, dependent upon individual karma.

Forget not that there are handicaps found in the astral and mental vehicles, as well as the physical, and that these, too, must be recognized, understood and put into right use.

In its larger aspect, this condition is planetary karma, the seeds of which were sewn long ago in a previous system. It manifests in the various kingdoms in nature (in proportion to the contributing factors associated with that kingdom) and in individuals according to their relative position within their kingdom; that is, their evolutionary status and previous choice.

What does this mean to student disciples? Very simply that their defects, whatever they may be, are the result of:

1. Previous choice as to the use made of the instrument.

2, Their evolutionary status, meaning that the instrument is a reflection in time and space of the incarnating consciousness, reflecting therefore, its growth and lack of growth.

3. Their service karma, which is a product of the above two, plus the service plan decided upon by the Soul, and this often entails sacrifice. In other words, a Soul may build a defective instrument in order to render a specific service. By taking on certain conditions, the more advanced consciousness can serve the race by eliminating the condition, as

such, from race mind consciousness, or more correctly, by transmuting the condition into its polar opposite. A distortion is transmuted into a perfection.

When this is the case, the disciples will be seen to be working, to be serving, because of, not in spite of, the handicap. The consciousness is so advanced that such ones are not apathetic, nor do they procrastinate. Think on this, my brothers.

All of these things have to be considered by the disciple as regards healing. All disciples are, to a greater or lesser degree, interested in the art of healing; often because of some difficulty of their own or one of a brother.

Once disciples realize what is really meant by Spiritual healing, much will be accomplished in the world of form, but it will not be done through undue attention to form. The attention has been given to the wrong aspect, that is, the correction of a physical defect, thus very little has been done of lasting value.

I would have you realize, my brother, that in every defect there is Divine Intent. Discover that intent and you will discover the means of correcting the defect. Do not look upon a form manifestation, regardless of its nature, as something which should not be. Realize that Divine Purpose underlies every appearance and that that Purpose is the evolution of consciousness.

The appearance of a defect in the instrument is but an indication of an area of consciousness into which the light of the Soul has not penetrated. Here there is darkness. What else but ignorance, my brothers? Through a process of meditation, acceptance and right use, the consciousness becomes the recipient of light and defect is corrected.

The Soul and Its Instrument

How is this done?

1. By recognizing the handicap, whatever it may be, as a part of the equipment with which you serve humanity.

2. By accepting that equipment as advantageous and opportune.

3. By meditating upon its Divine Intent or intended expression in line with Divine Purpose.

4. By putting it into right use, expressing its Divine Intent.

Please look to your own equipment. As an assignment, discover its defects, so-called, and arrive at an understanding of their Divine Intent. Hand in the written paper to your teacher.

PEACE BE UNTO YOU.

Lesson 18

Notes

_____

_____

_____

_____

_____

_____

_____

_____

_____

_____

_____

_____

_____

_____

_____

_____

_____

_____

The Soul and Its Instrument

Notes

_____

_____

_____

_____

_____

_____

_____

_____

_____

_____

_____

_____

_____

_____

_____

_____

_____

Lesson 18

Notes

How To Study
The Soul and Its Instrument

The Soul and Its Instrument is a course in self-initiated spiritual growth and development. It is designed to facilitate step-by-step unfoldment from individuality to group awareness and conscious service to the One Life. Each lesson in this course is a step in a transformative process. This process includes:

I.

A. Studying the Material: The information included in the course is presented in a cyclic fashion. Each lesson builds a foundation for understanding and prepares the way for the next lesson. This progression from one lesson to the next creates an harmonic rhythm which aids the transformation process.

In order to establish and maintain this rhythm, we suggest that all students of the course do the following:

1. Begin with Lesson 1 and study each lesson in turn. Skipping around or starting in the middle will break the rhythm and cause confusion.

2. Spend at least one week (seven days) studying each lesson. Begin a new lesson on the same day of a week. You may devote more than one week to each lesson, but if you do, spend the same number of weeks with each lesson.

3. While studying the course, concentrate your attention on the course. Avoid practicing internal exercises from other disciplines, as they may not combine well with the exercises in *The Soul and Its Instrument*.

The Soul and Its Instrument

We do not mean to imply that this course is in any way superior to any other course or discipline. In order to maintain the internal rhythm of this course, you must stay in the course. Once you have completed S.I. (*The Soul and Its Instrument*), we encourage you to include other schools and disciplines in your study and practice.

4. Complete the assignments. The structure of the course is similar to that of a textbook and includes frequent assignments. These assignments can be divided into three types:

   a. Subjective: These include internal activities such as the meditations.

   b. Objective: These include external activities such as writing a paper.

   c. Subjective and Objective: These combine internal and external activities in a single assignment (such as keeping a meditation log).

In each case, the assignment is there for a specific purpose, to help you expand your awareness or embody a new concept. Completing the assignments is part of the rhythm of the course.

B. Practicing the Meditation Techniques: The internal disciplines included in *The Soul and Its Instrument* are presented in a natural progression from basic to advanced. The meditations are the heart of the course; the information in the lessons is designed to aid your practice and comprehension of the meditations.

1. Practice each of the meditation techniques exactly as described.

2. Keep a meditation log: A daily written record helps you move the abstract realizations gained

in meditation into your outer life and affairs. Each entry should include the day and date, the meditation technique, and any noticeable results. Include all realizations and internal experiences which occur during the meditation, and any related insights and experiences which occur during the day or in your dreams.

3. Learn the meditation forms. Be patient with the process. Over time the results will become apparent. We encourage you to practice these techniques as an on-going process for your inner growth.

C. Embodying What You Learn: *The Soul and Its Instrument* course is designed to help you find your place, and take up your work, in the One Life. It does this through:

1. The Course of Instruction: This instruction consists of 18 lessons and lasts approximately four months. During this period you concentrate on learning the ideas, practicing the techniques, and making The Wisdom a part of your daily life and affairs. Studying the lessons and practicing the techniques begin the process of self-transformation. You complete that process as you apply your new understanding.

2. The Embodiment Cycle: The months of instruction are followed by a matching period of application. *The Soul and Its Instrument* course is completed by moving what you learn from the instruction beyond your immediate environment. This application or embodiment of The Wisdom includes:

a. Subjective activity: Most of your service will be subjective, and may include many of the techniques you learned in *The Soul and Its instrument* and its sister courses. If you continue to practice The Wisdom after completing the instruction, you will create an opportunity to help transform your environment.

b. Objective service: Your subjective practice may result in opportunities for providing objective service to family, friends, co-workers or environment.

II.

Because students often approach a new course with preconceptions based on previous experiences, keeping an open mind and an open heart will allow your intuition to integrate those experiences with the new material presented in the course.

There are a variety of methods of studying *The Soul and Its Instrument*. A positive approach is one which helps the student initiate his or her own growth and development. One method which is most supportive of self-initiation is Individual Self-directed Study.

Initiating your own spiritual growth and development means choosing a path of study, practice, and application which is right for you.

The primary value of individual, self-directed study lies in:

1. A stronger focus of will: Every time you decide to study a lesson, practice a technique, or do an assignment, you are exercising your will. As with any other kind of exercise, in order to receive the benefit you must do the work. No one can do it for you.

Appendix A

2. That process is described in this recommendation from *The Path of Initiation, Vol. II, lesson 4*:

"Many students reading this lesson will wonder how to do this work of lifting the polarization without direct contact with a teacher. I shall answer that question in several ways. Firstly, let us understand that all aspiring to the Soul are in direct contact with a teacher, namely their own Soul; and by continued aspiration, they will soon come to recognize the contact.

Secondly, aspirants are enabled, through their right aspiration, to contact higher levels of awareness, and from these levels draw down those concepts of Truth which provide a sure foundation for their later understanding.

Thirdly, aspirants learn to recognize experience as a great teacher, and through their efforts to live the Truth which they have grasped, they develop in the school of experience a consciousness rich in understanding. They do this deliberately, in full awareness of the activity, and their everyday life becomes a thing of beauty, regardless of appearances."

3. Self-initiated service: As you subjectively respond to the needs of your environment, you expand your awareness of your place and function in the One Life. This in turn leads to conscious service to that Life as you take your place in It.

III.

If you are considering teaching *The Soul and its Instrument*, we earnestly suggest that you first experience the course. Experiencing the course will help you:

A. Become aware of the difficulties attached to teaching. These include:

The Soul and Its Instrument

1. The sage on a stage: The idea of being a spiritual teacher can be very attractive. Often the idea is so attractive that seekers attempt to create the outer form without first achieving the inner content. This difficulty can be avoided by:

   a. Studying the course materials: You cannot teach what you do not know. Before you can facilitate the course, you must first experience it for yourself.

   b. Practicing what you learn: You cannot teach what you cannot perform. Before you can teach someone else the techniques, you must practice and perform them yourself. Example is the best form of teaching.

2. Being a "successful" teacher: This difficulty is based on the idea that an effective teacher has a classroom full of students. An effective teacher doesn't have to have a lot of students. Teaching is not a popularity contest. Such a focus turns the teacher's attention on the student and away from the Wisdom. Neither does teaching have to occur in a conventional classroom.

The Soul and Its Instrument is neither a treatise on The Ageless Wisdom nor a meditation manual. Only through right aspiration to the Soul and successful completion of all the materials and exercises will one truly know *The Soul and Its Instrument* and thus be qualified to assist others in their Self-initiated, Self-directed study.

Further Information

For further information on *The Soul and Its Instrument*, and related courses and materials, send a self-addressed, stamped envelope to: Further Information, Wisdom Impressions, P.O. Box 2008, Yucca Valley, CA 92286

INDEX

1st Ray—
  astral body, 167
  drive, 157
  identified, 166
  mental, 169
  mental body, 168
  Mind, 188
  power, 168
  power aspect, 130
  tends to isolate, 191
2nd Ray—
  identified, 166
  love aspect contacted, 131
  Soul, 167, 168, 169
  Wisdom aspect, contact via ajna, 129
3rd Initiation, 30—
  kundalini center lifted, 32
3rd Ray—
  identified, 166
  personality, 167
4th Ray—
  Astral, 169—
    vehicle, 191
  identified, 166
5th Ray—
  identified, 166
  mental body, 167
6th Ray—
  astral body, 168
  identified, 166
  personality, 169
  physical body, 167
7th Ray—
  coming in of, 191
  contemplate meaning, 170
  identified, 166
  karmic obligation, 191
  physical, 169
  physical magnetism, 190

A

Abstract Mind, definition, 99
Abstraction—
  clothe an, 40
  clothing, 98
  given concrete form, 98

into concrete form, 189
  takes concrete form, 100
Action, appearance of, 29
Activities—
  Daily, energy, 28
Activity, 18—
  all, 119
  nature of life, 16
  personality, 17
Affinity, phenomenon of Solar
  energy, 18
Ajna center—
  activated, 30
  and Head, interplay of energies, 129
  bridge to head center, 122
  contact the light, 129
  coordinator, 31
  Divine Love Wisdom, 32
  focus consciousness in, 33
  insight, 31
  located, 30
  Polarized in, acting as if, 129
  throws line to Soul, 122
Alignment—
  conscious, 119, 120
  definition, 120
  for expression of energies, 121
  head ajna throat, 31
  highest point of, 129
  of consciousness, focused in the
    ajna, 133
  of physical, emotional, mental, 7
  Soul mind and brain, 30
Animal, is aware of, 51
Animal soul, 40—
  definition, 39
Answers, to many problems, 179
Appearance, 32
Art, work of, 65
Ashram, pass on to, 152
Aspects, Three—
  component parts, 17
  each a triplicity, 17
  energy and motion, 18
  Major, 15, 17—
    human, 15
Aspirant—
  aspirational, 123

215

Index

Index

Divine, experience absorbed as
  Wisdom, 97
etheric body synthesizes, 51
Evolution of, 142, 152—
  etheric body, 28
evolution of your, 19
experiences, 19
extensions of, 108
focused in astral, 63
focused in mental, 7
Growth, in right direction, 75
Human—
  awareness of self, 16
  definition, 39
I, aspect of the Soul, 8
Identification, with vehicle, 108
identified with personality, 6
in pure state of being, 99
in the ajna, 134
in the plane of mind, 86
Incarnating—
  aware of purpose, 170
  development of, 169
  instrument, 199
inert, 152
inherent in, 152
inherent within form, 152
is not the, 96
liberation from form, 143
limitation of, 108
many states of, integration, 51
meaning part of, 95
mental body of, 98
Monadic, 15
moves into reality, 95
nature of life, 16
new, 152
not the entity, 95
of Soul, 97
of the One, 16
of the Soul, 179
Personality, 177—
  Consciousness, misnomer, 6
  polarized in mind, 119
  seat of, 121
  three states of, 51
Personality and Soul, blended, 122
project into vehicles, 152

projected, 7, 152, 187
purification of, 63
race mind, 19
recipient of light, 201
rock, 16
Shifting, entire lifetime, 86
slave to form, 8
Solar plexus, danger, 77
Soul and Personality, blended, 129
State of, definition, 51
steadily integrating, 189
subhuman, 40
Superhuman, 39—
  contact with, 39
the projected, 97
the result of, 96
three classifications, 39, 96
three states of, 151
ultimate synthesis, 51
unit of, 144
vegetable, 16
watches the cave, 134
when percentage shifted, 86
Constitution, of humanity, 15
Construction, threefold vehicle, 187
Contact, instrument of, 27
Contemplate—
  application, 8
  discipline, 8
  identification, 8
  meaning of 7 Rays, 170
Contemplation—
  meditative state, 27
  of the purpose of the form, 130
Continuity, 18
Cooperation, attitude of, 157
Cosmic awareness, 18
Cosmic consciousness, 99
Create, need to, 7
Creation, 18
Creative—
  Activity—
    experience of, 154
    impossible, 64
    of consciousness, 7
    Student, 7
  Art, service through, 76
  artist, 31

Index

Distortion, transmuted, 201
Divine—
  Energy, misdirection of, 179
  Expression, universal, 166
  Intelligence, 32
  Intent, expressing, 202
  Intention, 192—
    write understanding, 170
  Law and Order, 166
  Love—
    application of, 158
    for all, 87
    not an emotion, 87
    transmute resentments into, 178
    word impulsed by, 20
  Love-Wisdom, 32, 166—
    pouring through group instru-
      ment, 89
    meaning, 166
  Mind—
    above Divine Plan, 16
    definition, 99
    emanating from plane of, 100
    home of Monad, 16
    perfect form, 16
    perfect plan, 16
    perfect thought, 16
    plane, 16
    Plane of, formless, 99
  Prototype, conforming to, 75
  Purpose—
    aware of, 170
    evolution of consciousness, 201
    underlies every appearance, 201
  Will, 32—
    and Power, 166
Divine Plan—
  Divine Mind above, 16
  realization of, 170
  working out, 15
Divinity—
  essential, 141
  seven expressions of, 165
Doctrines, Eastern and Western, 191
Domination, freedom from, 41
dreamer, 41
Dreams, give form, 41
Duality, essential, 6

Dweller—
  in the body, 107
  merged with Soul, 108

E

Education, Scientific, 188
Egoic Egg, instrument of contact,
  151
Electrical, quality, 15
Electron, negative, 17
Emotion—
  definition, 86
  Human, force of, 73
  part of consciousness, 95
Emotional—
  Body, dominating, 167
  drive for power, 168
  energy, 19
  Interest, common, 156
  Nature—
    disciplines, 169
    inhibit, 64
  Relationship, limitation of, 156
  strength, 74
Emotions—
  gross, 76
  individual known by, 74
Endocrine glands, 29
Endurance, 188
Energies—
  Appropriated, purpose, 142
  centers of transmission, 29
  Classifications, four, 28
  disciple, 19
  governing environment, 28
  governing individual form, 28
  high vibratory frequency, 120
  misinterpreted, 19
  New, felt, 19
  planet, 29
  race, 28
  Soul, 19
  three-fold, 19
  to aspire, 31
  to seek, 31
  wrongly directed, 19

Index

Of—
- adultery, 153
- daughter, 153
- father, 153
- husband, 153
- incarnation, 154
- meditation, 154
- mother, 153
- murder, 153
- of creative activity, 154
- poverty, 153
- prostitution, 153
- rape, 153
- ruler, 153
- servant, 153
- slave, 153
- son, 153
- theft, 153
- war, 153
- wealth, 153
- wife, 153
- past, 191
- repeated, 179
- shared with brothers, 154

Experimentation—
- extreme care, 15
- lines indicated, 15
- sufficient information, 15

Extra Sensory Perception, 75—
- closes door, 64
- development of, 64

F

Faith, lack of, 187

Family—
- born into, 156
- energy, 28
- wish life, 73

Father—
- blessings of, 5
- dedicated to work of, 5
- The, return to, 153

Fear—
- conquered, 61
- of astral plane, 61

Flesh, ties of, 156

Flower, is aware of, 51

Force—
- centers, 29
- lines of, 28
- necessary to action, 29
- of Soul, 16
- physical, 29
- propulsion, 15
- repulsion, 17

Forces—
- control, 74
- converging, 73

Form, 32—
- Abstract, truth in, 64
- blinded by, 73
- Building, action that produces, 130
- conceived, 100
- concrete, 40
- consciousness in, 152
- consciousness within, 152
- Created, placing on the Om, 134
- determined by, 18
- distorted by, 100
- energies that govern, 28
- fluidic and solid, 100
- give life to, 131
- given separate astral existence, 131
- group expression, 158
- in three worlds, 100
- instrument of contact, 6
- integrated, 6
- Meaning, attempting to feel, 95
- Nature—
    - aspirant masters the, 8
    - limitations of, 152
    - positive control, 7
- Physical, incarnation in, 152
- prisoner to, 63, 152
- projection into astral, 130
- visualized in the cave, 133

Forms, many varied, 73

Formula, ascertained by Disciple, 130

Frequency, determines form, 18

Future, see into, 73

Index

Index

Index

Index

Index

Index

achieved wisdom, 179
align with, 33
and personality—
    battle between, 189
    mental battle, 189
animal, 40
animal or subhuman, 17
appropriates substance, 166
awaiting incarnation, 169
aware of, 6, 177, 187
awareness of relationship, 154
builds form, 166
Christ consciousness, 17
Consciousness—
    full, 177
    not possible, 8
    of, 153, 179
    three classifications, 39
construction of vehicle, 187
control of instrument, 177
cooperate with, 170
cooperating with, 187
creative aspect of, 7
definition, 16
desire body of, 76
desires life of, 87
devotion to, 188
early recognition, 188
energies, 19
equipment of, 165
Evolution of, conditions, 154
experience while incarnate, 6
family born into, 156
field of experience, 157
focuses itself into, 17
force, 16
guidance of, 100
habitat of, 99
Human, 17, 39, 151—
    beyond polarization, 153
I consciousness, 8
ideal, 75
identify with, 6
Incarnating, manifesting conditions, 153
independent of form, 6
inspired service, 76
Instrument—

of contact, 27
three-fold, 27
interpretation of Monadic impulse, 16
into the, 7
Karma, adjusted, 157
Laws of, 19
Liberated, born, 144
liberation from darkness, 154
Life of—
    attracted to, 121
    orienting to, 170
Light of, 88, 155—
    acceptance, 117
    has not penetrated, 201
    to brain, 158
line thrown to, 122
little chance, 167
lower consciousness merged
    with, 99
magnetic attraction, 17
meditation in the light, 180
motion, 16
Overshadowing, focused
    thought, 107
personality reoriented to, 117
preparing consciousness, 189
projected consciousness, 187
projects part of its consciousness, 6
Purpose vaguely aware of, 187
quality, 16
Ray, 165—
    2nd, 167
    2nd Ray, 168
    Love-Wisdom, 190
    makeup, 157
    way of least resistance, 167
reflects its light, 129
shift of polarization, 168
source of energy, 120
Spiritual, 17, 39, 151—
    in meditation, 97
    interest in affairs of personality, 97
super human, 17
they are the, 142
think of them as, 178
Tie, 156—

235

Index